A HERITAGE OF STONE

A HERITAGE OF STONE

BUILDINGS OF THE NIAGARA PENINSULA, FERGUS AND ELORA, GUELPH, REGION OF WATERLOO, CAMBRIDGE, PARIS, ANCASTER-DUNDAS-FLAMBOROUGH, HAMILTON AND ST. MARYS

NINA PERKINS CHAPPLE

James Lorimer & Company, Ltd.
Toronto

This book is dedicated to my loving family, Jerry, Alex, Sarah, Mala, and Zara.

James Lorimer & Company Ltd. acknowledges the support of the Ontario Arts Council. We acknowledge the support of the Government of Canada through the Book Publishing Industry Development Program (BPIDP) for our publishing activities. We acknowledge the support of the Canada Council for the Arts for our publishing program. We acknowledge the assistance of the OMDC Book Fund, an initiative of Ontario Media Development Corporation.

Cover design: Marilee MacKay

Library and Archives Canada Cataloguing in Publication

Chapple, Nina Perkins
    A Heritage of Stone : Buildings of The Niagara Peninsula, Fergus and Elora, Guelph, Region of Waterloo, Cambridge, Paris, Ancaster-Dundas-Flamborough, Hamilton and St. Marys and St. Marys / Nina Perkins Chapple.

Includes bibliographical references and index.
ISBN-13: 978-1-55028-935-0
ISBN-10: 1-55028-935-7

    1. Stone buildings--Ontario--History--19th century. 2. Architecture--Ontario--19th century. 3. Historic buildings--Ontario. I. Title.

NA746.O5C43 2006   721'.04410971309034   C2006-903621-7

James Lorimer & Company Ltd., Publishers
317 Adelaide Street West, Suite #1002
Toronto, ON
M5V 1P9
www.lorimer.ca

Printed and bound in China.

Photo Credits:

Cover images, clockwise from top left: Terry Manzo, Terry Manzo, Rob Skeoch, Rob Skeoch, Terry Manzo, Terry Manzo, Nina Perkins Chapple, Terry Manzo, Rob Skeoch.

Back Cover images, clockwise from top left: Rob Skeoch, Terry Manzo, Terry Manzo, Nina Perkins Chapple, Terry Manzo, Rob Skeoch, Rob Skeoch, Rob Skeoch, Terry Manzo.

L=left, R=right, T=top, B=bottom M=middle

Nina Perkins Chapple: 8 Middle Row Left, 8 Middle Row Middle, 31L, 32TL, 36TL, 36BL, 37R, 40, 42, 45TL, 46TR, 47TR, 52, 59BL, 60L, 61T, 61B, 62, 64BL, 68TR, 69T, 89TL, 92TL, 96L, 96TR, 102L, 102R, 103R, 105TL, 105BR, 106BL, 110L, 112TL, 114TR.

Terry Manzo: 8 Top Row Middle, 8 Top Row Right, 8 Bottom Row Right, 10L, 12R, 28, 30, 31R, 32BL, 32R, 33TR, 33BR, 34, 35TL, 35TR, 35BR, 38, 41L, 41TR, 41BL, 41BR, 43L, 43R, 44L, 44R, 45R, 46TL, 46BL, 47BR, 48TL, 48BL, 48TR, 48BR, 49L, 49R, 50L, 50BR, 51, 55TL, 55R, 56TL, 56BL, 57TL, 57TR, 58TL, 58BL, 59TL, 59TR, 64TL, 65R, 66L, 66R, 67TL, 67TR, 67BR, 68TL, 68BL, 69BR, 70, 71L, 71TR, 72, 73TR, 73BR, 108, 110TR, 111, 112BL, 113TL, 113TR, 113BR, 114TL, 115TL, 115TR, 116L, 117R.

Rob Skeoch: 5, 8 Bottom Row Left, 8Top Row Left, 8 Bottom Row Middle, 8 Middle Row Right, 12L, 13R, 14, 16, 17L, 17R, 18L, 18TR, 19TL, 19TR, 19BR, 20L, 20TR, 20BR, 21TR, 21BR, 22L, 22R, 23L, 23TR, 23BR, 24, 25, 26L, 26R, 27T, 27B, 74, 76TL, 76BL, 77TL, 77R, 78TL, 78TR, 79TL, 79TR, 79BR, 80TL, 80BL, 81TL, 81TR, 81BR, 82TL, 82TR, 82BL, 83TL, 83R, 84TL, 84BL, 85TL, 85TR, 85BR, 86, 88, 89TR, 90TL, 90TR, 91TR, 91BR, 92BL, 92TR, 93TL, 93TR, 93BR, 94TL, 94BL, 95TL, 95TR, 97TL, 97TR, 98, 100TL, 100BL, 101R, 103TL, 104L, 104TR, 105TR, 106TL, 107TR, 107BR.

Contents

Acknowledgements

For this book, I am indebted to the owners of stone buildings, public and private, who have generously shared their knowledge, welcomed a stranger, and spent years restoring and maintaining their heritage premises. Among others who were invaluable in the preparation of this book are the heritage planners for each municipality, the museum directors, historical societies, and local architectural conservation advisory committees (LACACs), dedicated professionals and volunteers who are a storehouse of knowledge about local architecture.

For the Niagara Peninsula, Leah Wallace, Heritage Planner for the Municipality of Niagara, and Restoration Architect Peter John Stokes provided valuable information on the area, as did Clark Bernat, Managing Director of the Niagara Historical Society and Museum, and Arden Phair, Curator of Collections at the St. Catharines Museum. Laura Dodson of the School of Restoration Arts shared research on Willowbank, and Marilynn Havelka, Chief Administrative Officer, did the same for Ruthven Park. Barry and Linda Coutts gave a tour of their restored home, and Bob Watson identified the use of local sandstone in Queenston.

In Fergus and Elora, writer Steve Thorning, Linda Lonsdale of the Township of Centre Wellington, Eleanor Smith and Don Fraser of Heritage Centre Wellington, and the archivists at the Wellington County Museum and Archives were very helpful in introducing me to sites and sources of information. Wayne and Joan Prowse provided a tour of their home, and the Reverend Kees Vandermey, minister at the Knox Presbyterian Church in Elora, sent a historical account of the building of the church.

Guelph yielded an abundance of resources. Archivist Linda Amichand and her staff provided access to the Gordon Couling Collection, an enormously valuable holding on Ontario stone architecture in the Archival and Special Collections at the University of Guelph. Ian Panabaker, Urban Designer and Heritage Planner with the City of Guelph, supplied me with extensive research on local designated buildings. Katherine McCracken, Director of Guelph Museums, provided material on the McCrae House, and home owner Elton Yerex updated me with the latest facts about his heritage house.

Margaret and Bob Rowell of the Architectural Conservancy of Ontario, North Waterloo Branch, generously provided a driving tour along the back roads of Waterloo County and pointed out the wonderful resource of Mennonite farmhouses there. Planners Leon Bensason of Kitchener, Danielle Ingram of the City of Waterloo, along with Larry Devitt, Director of Recreation for the Township of Woolwich, and the Heritage Wilmot Committee, Township of Wilmot, supplied much-needed data on local buildings. The staff in the Grace Schmidt Room of the Kitchener Public Library was very helpful in providing material. Bob and Dale Woolner gave me a tour of their home which they have carefully restored, and Linda and Jim Taleski offered a fascinating history of their house.

For Cambridge, my appreciation goes to Valerie Spring, Heritage

Planner for the City of Cambridge, who shared her considerable knowledge and gave me many leads, and to Michael Stacey of McDougall Cottage for his assistance.

The Paris Historical Society, Margaret Deans (who owns a fine cobblestone house), Pat Hasler-Watts, and planner Mark Pomponi with the County of Brant have all been valuable sources on the subject of Paris buildings. My thanks go to Nancy Sewell and Frank Inksater for helpful information and to Douglas Stocks for a tour of his splendid home.

In the Ancaster, Dundas, and Flamborough area, dedicated volunteers and professionals have built up a sound base of information on the area. Of particular assistance were Sylvia Wray, Archivist of the Flamborough Archives, and Elizabeth Toews of Dundas. Elizabeth and Jim Combs, Elizabeth and John Heersink, and Jacqueline and Oliver Wesley-James showed me through their beautifully restored homes. Dr. Alvin Lee and Dr. Peter Marsales were generous in sharing information about their properties.

In Hamilton, architect Anthony Butler and Jean and Sandy McKay, long-time supporters of heritage conservation, gave assistance that was greatly appreciated.

St. Marys Museum and Archives curator Mary Smith allowed me to peruse the research files which proved very useful; Paul King provided good advice; Lorne Eedy recounted his family's long-term publishing association with the town; and Denise Fergusson gave me a delightful tour of her cottage.

Finally, I would like to thank, in particular, three people who have experience, and time to this book: Dr. Gerard Middleton, Professor Emeritus of Geology, McMaster University, who has served informally as the technical expert on the identification of building stone; Emily Cain, who has been a continuous source of encouragement throughout the project; and my husband, Jerry Chapple, who has loyally served as first reader, steadfast supporter, and general helper in a multitude of ways.

Introduction

Stone has always been considered the most prestigious building material. The pyramids and temples of antiquity and the great cathedrals and palaces of medieval Europe have firmly established the tradition that stone was the prime choice for building great monuments. Compared to brick and wood, stone is by far the oldest building material. The sedimentary (layered) stone of southwestern Ontario—limestone and sandstone—was formed as long ago as 385 million years, while the igneous (once molten) granite fieldstone is millions of years older. We live, work, and worship inside these buildings of stone with hardly a thought given to their primordial origins. Stone buildings hold a special attraction, a fascination with their ageless quality, strength, and endurance, and with the natural beauty of the stone itself.

As the strongest and most permanent building material, stone was traditionally used for important, large-scale engineering projects. At the beginning of the nineteenth century, when British North America was just opening up for settlement, stone was frequently chosen for building new transportation and defense systems. Britain sent numbers of skilled stonemasons to the colony to work on such substantial masonry projects as the British Naval Yards in Kingston (1820), the Rideau Canal (1832), and Kingston's Fort Henry (1833). Stonemasons were also in demand for building the Erie Canal (1825) and the second Welland Canal (1845). The next demand came during the building of the railroads in the early 1850s as stonemasons were

Fieldstone was the masonry preferred by the Mennonite settlers of Waterloo, as illustrated in this side view of the Swope House in West Montrose.

sent out across the province to erect massive masonry viaducts and retaining walls. It was then that these stonemasons learned about communities that promised future work.

The timing was ideal for a sudden boom in stone buildings. Railways brought the promise of future growth, and the citizens of flourishing young communities were poised to transform their villages of pioneer wooden buildings into solid, ageless, stone streetscapes reminiscent of their homelands. Original settlers had acquired sufficient wealth; local governments were firmly established; and prosperity attracted more immigrants, including well-trained stonemasons primarily from the British Isles and Ireland. (By comparison, few masons came from America because building in stone was relatively rare during this era, being limited primarily to upper New York state and Pennsylvania.) In Ontario, the stone buildings erected during this transformative period of the 1850s to the 1870s include some of the most notable structures ever built in the province.

When I set out on my quest for stone buildings in southwestern Ontario, I discovered it was the landscape itself (the geography and the geology) that determined where building in stone became prolific. Although the region sits on bedrock, stone for quarrying generally became accessible by the action of watercourses over the millennia as they cut their way down through the rock, or by the gradual upheaval of the Earth's crust as in the formation of the Niagara Escarpment. Quarried stone consisted of various forms of sandstone and limestone (the latter is the term used generally in architecture; geologists break it down more specifically to limestone, dolomitic limestone, and dolomite). In southwestern Ontario, stone quarries appeared along the Grand, Speed, and Thames Rivers and along the Niagara Escarpment, starting where it rises out of the Niagara River at Queenston, and concentrating around the head of Lake Ontario. Because stone was not easily transported, stone towns developed where the stone was quarried.

Fieldstone, including granite from the Canadian Shield, was left scattered across the landscape by glaciers as they retreated 10,000 years ago. Because of its widespread occurrence in the countryside, fieldstone became a favourite building material for rural farmhouses and, occasionally, for entire barn buildings, not just the foundations. Supply as well as the ethnic background of the settlers largely determined where fieldstone buildings appeared. The stone, identified for each building in the text, refers to the walls of the principal façades. Rubblestone was commonly used in back and side walls.

The subject—stone buildings of southwestern Ontario—casts a wide net and catches an amazingly rich resource—literally thousands of stone buildings of all types. The 114 examples chosen for this book represent only a small fraction of stone architecture found in the area. While masonry structures are often well-known and even revered in their own hometowns, knowledge of their counterparts in other southwestern Ontario localities is limited. The book breaks new ground by introducing the reader to a broad overview of communities that were building in stone, all around the same time. As a result, the material for each area must be limited to a brief sample. This general approach, on the other hand, allows us to include all building types—whether houses, town halls, churches, commercial blocks, or industrial buildings—located in all types of settlements, from the small village to the large urban area. The purpose is to entice the reader to explore further, to discover the timeless beauty and skilled craftsmanship of these works in stone.

Choosing 114 representative buildings from the thousands of candidates meant narrowing the focus to a few prime elements. First, the buildings had to be built in local—not imported—stone because this embodies quite literally the natural, indigenous character of the site. Second, buildings in concentrated numbers (i.e., settlements) were preferred because, collectively, they could build a picture of a place, its character, and identity. (This decision unfortunately ruled out most of the historic fieldstone farmhouses and small hamlets that beautify the Ontario countryside.) Lastly, communities of different ethnic backgrounds—Scottish, English, and German—were chosen because masonry techniques show an amazing variety from place to place, according to the cultural heritage of the settlers. For each criterion,

Squared limestone masonry is used in Inglebrook.

Both the Ohio sandstone, used on the Hamilton Custom House (left) and the local limestone used on the Guelph City Hall (right) can be more easily carved than most limestones.

though, there are exceptions; for example, the Mennonite farmhouses of Waterloo are obviously not in an urban area, but, more importantly, they articulate clearly their Pennsylvania-German heritage.

Perhaps the strongest message that comes out of this broad approach is the surprising degree of regional variation in stone architecture, even between nearby towns. These variations grew in part out of the difference of the local stone itself and how it was used. Stone buildings disclose all sorts of information about their makers: give clues to their origins: the Mennonites of Waterloo preferred unshaped natural fieldstone collected off their land and laid randomly in a wall, using an ample supply of mortar for support. Settlers in the Scottish settlements of Fergus and Galt built structures of squared stone, fitted tightly together in rows with relatively little mortar, often hammer-dressed (not smooth), and usually with little or no added decoration. On the other hand, Guelph's amber-grey limestone could be tooled or carved into an elaborate array of pedimental or segmental lintels and beautiful console brackets, similar to the ornamental work in Hamilton, which was sculpted in sandstone from the escarpment. Each community, too, had its own sense of identity, that would be expressed in its architecture.

In every community, certain personalities became prominent because of their impact on their towns: the Elora Mill would not have existed without the indefatigable Scot, J. M. Fraser; St. Marys might have been slower to develop without the civilizing efforts of the Hutton family; Paris might never have acquired its legacy of cobblestone buildings if the American Levi Boughton had not come to town; and Guelph would have looked different without the remarkable talents of the English stonecarver Matthew Bell.

The stonemasons, carvers, and quarrymen are the real heroes of this story, but, unfortunately, information about their lives and work is sparse. These masons would also have had strong views on the appropriate mortar and pointing techniques to use. Because historic stone buildings have been repointed numerous times over the years, identifying the generations of stonemasons have added their own style of pointing over the years to a building, investigation into original mortar warrants an in-depth study of its own. (Owners of stone buildings should be warned against repointing in hard Portland cement—it can cause deterioration of the stone due to the freeze-thaw cycle.)

To put it in a larger context, the stone architecture of Quebec that had begun centuries earlier and culminated in such beautiful places as Montreal and Quebec City is deservedly well known, as are the stone buildings of eastern Ontario, found in Kingston, Ottawa, and Perth among other places. The stone legacy of southwestern Ontario, however, is still to be fully discovered. Collectively, this splendid heritage is an important dimension of the province's architectural resources. Perhaps our present-day eyes do not always see the subtle varieties in the masonry, or the art in the stone carvings, or the beauty in the proportions that our forebearers did. Every stone building is different; clues to its time, place, and builder are embedded in its fabric. It is well worth the time to take a second look. These buildings have their own stories to tell, if we listen.

Cobblestone was a specialized form of masonry used in Paris before Confederation.

The Niagara Peninsula

The Niagara Peninsula introduces the story of building in stone in southwestern Ontario, just as it opened the way for the earliest pioneers to settle the land. Many of the first arrivals were fleeing for their lives across the Niagara River following the American Revolution. Some belonged to the Butler's Rangers, and some were half-pay British soldiers, while many others were Loyalists from American colonies who wanted to live under the British Crown. Dispossessed of their homes, lands, and personal belongings, refugees were welcomed and given free land on the Niagara Peninsula in return for their allegiance. Britain actively encouraged this settlement to demonstrate its control and to deter American expansion.

The Niagara Purchase of 1781 authorized the transfer of land near the Niagara River to the British from the Mississauga First Nation, thereby opening up the area to the first of the United Empire Loyalists. In 1791, Britain officially established Upper Canada (Ontario) and appointed Colonel John Graves Simcoe to govern the colony. In 1792, Newark (now called Niagara-on-the-Lake) became the capital of Upper Canada, developing into a flourishing British headquarters right at the entry point to the western frontier. In 1796, the capital was moved to York (now called Toronto), and in 1798, Newark was renamed Niagara. As the soldiers and Loyalists came through Newark searching for a new home, the government gave them large tracts of land, primarily along the coasts of Lake Ontario and Lake Erie as well as along rivers and near the spiny ridge of the Niagara Peninsula where

Left: Willowbank, designed by architect John Latshaw and built in 1834–1836, is an exuberant Greek Revival showpiece. This Queenston property belonged to Alexander Hamilton's family for 100 years. It was recently rescued from demolition by a citizens' group and is now the School of Restoration Arts.

Above and facing page: Nelles Manor, built in 1798 in Grimsby, may be the oldest substantial stone house in southwestern Ontario. The Nelles home escaped destruction during the War of 1812 and was large enough to host the end-of-the-war celebrations.

a trail used by the Native peoples ran. Traditionally, primitive log cabins or wood shanties for basic shelter were built first, followed by a mill or barn for economic survival. However, by the early 1800s, substantial houses began to appear in the wilderness, some even built of stone, which was rather surprising given the need for specialized masonry skills. These structures were almost invariably located close to the source of the stone.

The buildings of the Niagara Peninsula chosen for inclusion represent those pre-dating the late-1840s; by the 1850s British-trained stonemasons began arriving in numbers throughout southwestern Ontario, instigating a full-fledged movement in stone architecture that is the subject of this book. These earlier structures, however, tell a special story—that of taming and civilizing the wild frontier. During its first half century, the Niagara Peninsula was a place of great promise, but also of considerable vulnerability. Transportation by water was a prime asset with transshipment points at Niagara and Queenston that were later bypassed by the construction of the first and second Welland Canals (wood in 1829 and stone in 1845), considered one of the great engineering feats of pre-Confederation Canada. Water power was abundant, fuelled by the many creeks that tumbled down the escarpment. The stone of the Niagara Escarpment proved suitable for building and making lime for mortar. This early period, however, was still unstable. The new immigrants, who had already suffered the hardships of the Revolutionary War, were to experience them again during the War of 1812. American troops marched up the peninsula to Stoney Creek, occupied and then burned the settlement at Niagara when retreating in 1813. The peoples of the Six Nations Confederacy, recently resettled along the Grand River, continued to support the British side under the leadership of Chief Joseph Brant. Another conflict was feared in 1837 when troops mustered at Queenston to fend off William Lyon Mackenzie and his followers who were threatening an attack that abruptly fizzled.

Given these unsettled times, it is all the more remarkable that many of the stone buildings erected during this pre-1850 era showed an

exceptionally high level of craftsmanship and refinement that seems at odds with the relatively primitive state of settlement. One of the earliest military families who acted as intermediaries between the British and Native peoples during the Revolutionary War was that of Colonel Robert Nelles. He and his father, both working for the British Department of Indian Affairs, had escaped across the border in the early 1780s. They were rewarded for their role in the Indian raids along the Mohawk Valley with land on the Grand River. By 1787, Robert, at age twenty-six and married, founded his own settlement at Forty Mile Creek (now Grimsby, forty miles or sixty-four kilometres from the Niagara River). In the spirit of the landed gentry of his ancestors, Robert built in 1798 the Nelles Manor in the full-blown, traditional Georgian style, impressively large at two-storeys high and five bays wide, and constructed in the most permanent of building materials—stone, a local reddish escarpment sandstone. Typically, this ledge stone was thin and unshaped and would be laid uncoursed and

Above and right: Brown-Jouppien House, built from 1796–1810, is located near Twelve Mile Creek (west of St. Catharines). The present owners have carefully restored this well-proportioned limestone home, with painted floors and stencilling on the walls.

often covered with a thin coat of rough-cast, incised to imitate the more upscale ashlar. It must have been a stunning sight to emerge from the wilderness and suddenly encounter the elegant, civilized presence of the Nelles Manor. As Colonel Nelles grew more prosperous, he took on the role of magistrate and provincial representative, often providing counsel and shelter to the Native peoples whose language he spoke. It is said that on many a cold winter's night a Native person would slip in through the back kitchen door, sleep by the fire overnight, and leave quietly at dawn.

Another military man, John Brown, a private in the formidable Butler's Rangers, had fled across the Niagara River with his family in 1784, and by 1796 was settled in the backlands of Twelve Mile Creek (his rank as a private had not earned him a privileged location-ticket for waterfront property). The nearby escarpment yielded the limestone for his substantial, two-storey, five-bay home, the Brown-Jouppien House, begun in 1796 and finished by his sons in 1810. Its location on the old "stage road" from Niagara to Dundas established it as a stagecoach stop and tavern (a section of a birdcage bar is still in place). The Browns also

St. Mark's Anglican Church in Niagara-on-the-Lake was built by 1810 with sandstone brought to the site by troops stationed there under Major-General Isaac Brock, a parishioner. The stone walls survived a fire during the War of 1812; the damaged roof and interior were reconstructed by 1822.

incorporated fine craftsmanship into their house, as seen in the masonry as well as the decorative panelling and moulding in the interior. Erected in the bush, this handsome, unadorned, yet gracefully welcoming stone house even today looks out onto 1,700 acres of undeveloped land (now protected as the Short Hills Provincial Park).

Niagara served as a flourishing urban centre in these opening years of settlement. However, one of the devastating losses in the War of 1812 occurred on December 10, 1813, when American troops set fire to the town as they retreated. The sturdy, stone walls of St. Mark's Anglican Church, however, survived. Built by 1810, it was one of the earliest Anglican churches in the province. Among its parishioners were the British elite, including Major-General Isaac Brock. During

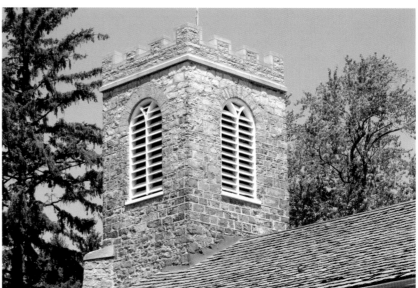

Details and interior of St. Mark's Anglican Church.

the War of 1812, the new church was immediately pressed into service, first as a hospital for British soldiers, and then as a barracks for American troops. After the war, the congregation struggled to come to terms with the destruction to the town, the loss of their beloved military leader, Brock, and the repairs to the church's roof and interior. By 1822, the structure was rebuilt; it was consecrated in 1828, and expanded eastward in 1843 with a transept and chancel. Under the later Gothic additions (the Gothic Revival had become the definitive style for churches in the later nineteenth century), the original three-bay wide, four-bay long, Neoclassical structure can still be detected in the rock-faced Whirlpool sandstone and the gracefully arched windows with their sixteen neatly fitted voussoirs. Today, a restored St. Mark's stands peacefully in a pastoral setting beside its original cemetery, a silent witness to those war years long ago.

At the point where the Niagara Escarpment rises out of the Niagara River, a small community formed, founded ca.1788 by the Scot entrepreneur, the Honourable Robert Hamilton. There, at Queenston, Hamilton built a wharf, storehouse, and stone residence (destroyed accidentally during the War of 1812), and embarked on an immensely successful career as merchant, judge, and legislative councillor that made him Niagara Peninsula's wealthiest settler by the time of his death in 1809. By the early 1820s, Queenston was serving as a military base, shipping depot, and post office (1808). The community of five hundred residents had as many as sixty homes, some of which were constructed in sandstone from nearby quarries. Yeoman William Davis from Massachusetts erected a handsome stone residence, the Davis-Prest House ca. 1819 that captured the very essence of the Loyalist style: five bays wide and two-storeys high with a central, semi-elliptical fanlight doorway. Exceptional for a farmhouse of this era is its sophisticated design and refined craftsmanship—mantelpieces were exquisitely carved with rosettes and reeding (attributed to skilled shipwrights who were over-wintering), and exterior walls were built of squared and coursed rock-faced sandstone on all four sides (the exception to the standard practice of rubblestone

The Davis-Prest House in Queenston was built ca. 1821 on the rising slope of the escarpment. A quarry near the owner's house supplied the Whirlpool sandstone for construction.

Davis-Elder House was built ca. 1821 by William Davis, apparently for his son. William Jr.'s house is beautifully situated under large chestnut trees with the added charm of stone lion hitching posts in front.

side and back walls). Set on a height of land, this restrained, well-proportioned residence has all the dignity and quiet beauty of its clapboard counterparts in New England. Next door, Davis erected a second stone house, the Davis-Elder House, built ca. 1821, thought to be for his son, also named William. Five bays wide, but smaller at one-and-a-half storeys, William Jr.'s house sits on rising land. As does the Davis Sr. home, the son's more modest home displays elements of fine craftsmanship seen in the closely fitted masonry, the stone end-chimneys, and the wood carving of the mantelpiece. It is difficult to imagine that these pastoral farmlands and fine homes occupied land that only a few years earlier had been under military siege. Another stately stone house of similar proportions was built nearby ca. 1819 overlooking the Niagara River, the Mackenzie House, named for its firebrand tenant, William Lyon Mackenzie. It was while living in this house that Mackenzie printed the first issue of his newspaper, the *Colonial Advocate,* on May 18, 1824. The success of the paper marked

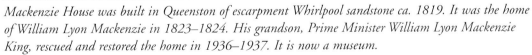

Mackenzie House was built in Queenston of escarpment Whirlpool sandstone ca. 1819. It was the home of William Lyon Mackenzie in 1823–1824. His grandson, Prime Minister William Lyon Mackenzie King, rescued and restored the home in 1936–1937. It is now a museum.

a turning point in his life, leading Mackenzie to embark on a lifelong mission of attacking the powerful Family Compact and passionately advocating reform. His career included his election as the first Mayor of Toronto, his leadership of the ill-fated Rebellion of 1837, twelve

Right: Willowbank's doorway illustrates the fine craftsmanship and Greek Revival detailing of its original (east façade) entrance.
Facing page: Willowbank's original rear façade with its raised first storey serves remarkably well as today's front façade.

years of exile, and finally again as a member of Parliament following his pardon in 1849. The Mackenzie house reveals its early date in the use of the Loyalist fanlight window and the twelve-over-twelve window panes of the first floor.

The most spectacular of all the Queenston stone houses is Willowbank built in 1834–1836 for Alexander Hamilton, the town's sheriff and postmaster and son of Queenston's founder, Robert. Willowbank captures the essence of the Greek Revival style, with its colossal (two-storey) colonnade and hilltop setting suggestive of an ancient classical temple in the landscape. Architect John Latshaw (from Drummondville, now Niagara Falls) designed the home on the grand scale–windows, doorways, columns, and hallways all have stunningly generous proportions that create an unusually bright and gracious interior. Behind the magnificent frontispiece of wooden columns stands a solid structure of squared, coursed local sandstone, typically rock-faced and relatively small. (Some limestone was used on the rear

Above and right: Ruthven, also designed by John Latshaw, was built on the Grand River near Cayuga in 1845–1846. This exemplary Greek Revival mansion and grounds stayed in the Thompson family until recently and is now being restored as Ruthven Park National Historic Site.
Facing page: The award-winning restoration of Ruthven's Coach House was completed in 2005, west façade above and east façade below.

façade.) With this building, Alexander Hamilton left his permanent imprint on the community, reflecting his family's privileged position, the era's close cultural ties with America (the Greek Revival style was particularly an American fad symbolizing the free republic), and the sophisticated level of craftsmanship and taste that this young country could achieve. Built to be the best, Willowbank counts among the finest Greek Revival country homes in Canada.

About ten years later, an equally splendid Greek "temple," designed by the same architect, John Latshaw, was built by Lieutenant-Colonel David Thompson. Ruthven, built in 1845–1846, is sited on the lower Grand River. From the same hometown as Latshaw, the adventurous entrepreneur Thompson must have been familiar with, and inspired by, his work. Similar to Willowbank, Ruthven displays a two-storey columned entrance portico, this time in the Doric style, which transformed the country house into a classical masterpiece. As the centrepiece of a 1,500-acre estate, Ruthven was designed in the tradition of the British gentleman's country estate, where grounds were laid out in picturesque fashion with a coach house, a carriageway, stables, gardens, and a long, winding entrance drive. Thompson, a member of Parliament, partner in the Grand River Navigational Company, and former contractor for the Welland Canal, showed his entrepreneurial spirit by importing the finest ashlar limestone from Sandusky, Ohio, for the main façades. Brought on scows, six at a time, towed by paddleboats across Lake Erie and up through Thompson's own Grand River canal system right to his property, this imported stone marks an exception to the rule of using local material. (Toronto, without its own local source, regularly imported stone.) The beautiful, smooth masonry and carved wooden architectural details found in the portico, the drawing room, and handsome oval staircase give direct proof of the sophisticated level of taste and lifestyle that could be achieved even in this pioneer era on the Niagara Peninsula. For both Alexander Hamilton and David Thompson, their homes became their legacy; sadly, neither lived longer than five years after his home was completed.

In the late 1840s, British stonemasons began arriving in large numbers in southwestern Ontario, and other masons became available once the Welland Canal was completed in 1845, so that a whole new movement of building in stone unfolded over the following decades. The Niagara Peninsula also had its share of fine stone buildings during this later era—courthouses (Niagara, St. Catharines, and Simcoe), churches, mills, and houses, especially in the communities along the escarpment, such as Thorold, Merritton, and St. Catharines. However, it was these pre-1850 stone structures of the Niagara Peninsula that set the stage for the ensuing movement; in the best cases, their quality remained unsurpassed.

Fergus and Elora

Situated on the upper Grand River just four kilometres apart, Fergus and Elora have shared a common background, but have been traditionally arch-rivals. Now they are amalgamated into a new political entity, Centre Wellington. Both were founded in the 1830s by adventurous Scottish entrepreneurs. Their grand schemes included purchasing vast areas of unbroken forest in Upper Canada and establishing new communities at the best water-power sites available, a movement modelled after the eighteenth-century Scottish "new towns." Adam Fergusson and James Webster, both gentleman farmers, founded a village site at "Little Falls" called Fergus in 1833. It was intended to be an exemplary Scottish-Canadian settlement for their 7,300-acre portion of Nichol Township. Captain William Gilkison, also a Scot, founded Elora in 1832 as part of his 14,000-acre purchase in the same township. Both settlements developed where the Grand River cascaded down through narrow gorges, providing excellent water power for industries and a beautiful setting for establishing a new life in the wilderness. Both communities made use of limestone near the surface and developed stone quarries along the riverbanks that yielded a supply of building stone and mortar.

On one hand, the founders of Fergus invested personally in the settlement; Fergusson actively sought out "carefully selected Scottish immigrants who possessed money and education." On the other hand, the premature death of Captain William Gilkison one year after founding Elora left the new settlement bereft of a driving force and his

Left: Rosemount Cottage, built in the early 1870s in the Italianate Revival style, rivals any of its Elora contemporaries with its beautifully carved sculptures that crown the front entrance and window heads. Rosemount Cottage previously served as a private school and is again a private home.

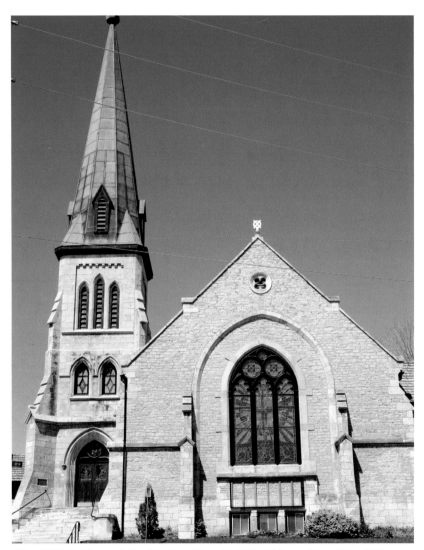

The 1862 St. Andrew's Presbyterian Church, designed by architect David Murray of Guelph, has a high nave and buttressed corner tower. The masonry combines the small, rough-faced Fergus stone with the lighter, smooth Guelph stone.

generous private support. By the 1850s, both villages had begun to grow, just when local limestone had become readily available and skilled stonemasons had arrived searching for work. It was during the following decades that Fergus gradually came of age as a "stone town": stores; churches; industries; stables; liveries; dwellings large and small— buildings of all types—were constructed in stone. Fergus still is remarkable for its wealth of stone architecture, attributable in part to its citizens' common Scottish heritage and in part to the abundant supply of local stone and the presence of skilled masons. Fergus today is said to have a resource of two hundred stone buildings.

By 1858, with a population of about 1,000, Fergus had grown large enough to be incorporated as a village and prosperous enough to begin the transformation from a pioneer outpost to a substantial downtown. While industries served as the economic catalyst for several decades following the mid-century mark, the long-term sustainability of this market town has depended on its business district. In the second half of the nineteenth century, substantial stone commercial blocks, two and three storeys high, gradually replaced the early frame buildings on St. Andrew Street West until a near-continuous streetscape of stone row buildings was formed, extending from St. David Street four blocks west to Breadalbane Street. Among the first to be built in 1858 was the Argo Block, a beautifully constructed, three-storey limestone block that is characteristic of the mid-century Classical Revival phase. As new stone blocks filled in the streetscape, each related to the other, but also added its own personality into the mix: gable or mansard roofs; two or three storeys high; and arches or pediments or both. By the 1880s, sandstone from the Credit Valley became the building material of choice, transported along a new rail connection to Cataract that opened in 1879. As seen in the 1883 Marshall Block, these High Victorian sandstone buildings injected a new sense of exuberance and drama to the more traditional limestone streetscape. Collectively, the business district of Fergus offers a delightful variety of Victorian Era fashions.

During this same period, several churches designed in the Gothic Revival style and constructed in stone also made their appearance in

Fergus, including St. Joseph's Roman Catholic Church in 1865 and the Melville United Church (formerly Free Presbyterian) in 1900. In a Scottish town such as Fergus, however, it was the established Presbyterian Church that took precedence. The first one built (a frame structure in 1834) was situated on a prestigious hilltop site at the head of James Square. Less than three decades later, the Auld Kirk re-asserted its prominence by erecting a new St. Andrew's Presbyterian Church on the same site in 1862. Constructed in limestone and designed in the full-

Left: The smooth, tightly fitted ashlar blocks and elegant carving around the windows of the 1858 Argo Block set high standards for the transformation of Fergus's main street into a downtown of handsome stone buildings.
Right: The Marshall Block, built in Fergus in 1883, capitalized on the new availability of Credit Valley sandstone and features the Second Empire style in its octagonal corner tower, mansard roof, and decorative dormers.

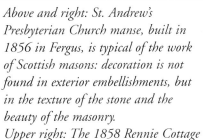

Above and right: St. Andrew's Presbyterian Church manse, built in 1856 in Fergus, is typical of the work of Scottish masons: decoration is not found in exterior embellishments, but in the texture of the stone and the beauty of the masonry.

Upper right: The 1858 Rennie Cottage of Fergus was first owned by William Rennie, a farmer-turned-builder, and is one of seven similar neighbouring houses. Built in the Ontario Cottage style, it represents a building form of pleasing proportions that was popular among skilled workers.

blown Gothic Revival style, the new structure featured a corner tower and broach spire that still reigns over the town below.

Typically the original houses in Fergus were of log construction, but the first stone house in town is said to have been constructed in 1840. Starting in the 1850s, a mix of stone homes began to appear; often the larger ones populated the higher slopes while the smaller, one-storey cottages were usually built near the Grand River. A beautiful old home built in 1856, St. Andrew's manse represents the early phase of stone house building in Fergus. The residence has a gracious presence and captures the very essence of fine proportions and simplicity of line, characteristic of this period. By contrast, the 1868 Rennie Cottage located near the river represents the one-storey Ontario Cottage style: modest in size and popular among skilled craftsmen and labourers. Typical characteristics are the hip roof and central entrance, with a nod to the Italianate style detected in the doorway's arches and colonnettes. The historic residential sections of town reveal a splendid array of house styles, shapes, and sizes that were built of stone throughout the nineteenth century. Successful merchants tended to favour the south side of the river, building grand homes with handsome landscaped gardens, many of which still exist.

On September 13, 1870, the Great Western Railway began regular service in Fergus, completing the connection from Hamilton via Guelph and Elora. At the rousing opening-day ceremony, sponsor Adam Brown from Hamilton predicted "the banks of your beautiful river will soon be musical with the hum of busy industry." The railroad did attract new industries to town, both water-powered and later steam-powered. Among the notable industries of Fergus were a sewing machine factory, a brewery, planing mill, Watson's Tannery at the bridge, James Wilson's Monkland Mills — famous for its production of oatmeal (which was exported to Scotland) — and the 1879 Beatty Brothers Foundry located by the river in the heart of town (now a popular retail centre called the Fergus Market). These last three buildings still exist, and all have been adapted to new uses. Typical of the large-scale nineteenth-century industrial structures, the foundry was constructed of local limestone and heavily mortared; the windows were over-sized to let in natural light; and the building was strictly functional with no applied decoration. Similar to other small towns of the Grand River valley, Fergus's industrial boom was subject to fire, flooding, and, in some cases, a general over-production (at one point sewing machines sold for as little as $10.00 each.) By the end of the nineteenth century, the town still possessed a few industries, including the Monkland Mills and the Beatty Brothers, enterprise, but was evolving basically into a rural market centre.

Neither Fergus nor Elora has major historic county buildings; however, located between the two villages is a prestigious public building that was the former Wellington County House of Industry

The Beatty Brothers Foundry of Fergus was built on the banks of the Grand River in 1879. It forms a striking industrial complex of connected structures, distinguished by its tall chimney stack and massive stone-gabled structure.

The 1877 House of Industry and Refuge, a National Historic Site, was designed by Guelph architect Victor Stewart in the Italianate Revival style. Noteworthy are its prominent belfry tower and rough-faced limestone construction. It now serves as the Wellington County Museum and Archives.

and Refuge, built in 1877. The plaque honouring its recognition as a National Historic Site explains just how rare a building it is in Canada today: it is "the earliest surviving example of an important nineteenth-century institution—the government-supported poorhouse". Its survival may be partly attributed to its appearance—a handsome stone structure that looks more like a Victorian school than a Dickensian poorhouse—and to its beautiful hilltop setting in the rolling countryside of the Grand River valley. Its conversion into the Wellington County Museum and Archives in the 1970s is recognized as a model project for surplus public buildings worthy of saving.

Compared to Fergus, growth in Elora was more measured. Most of its stone buildings were erected before the late 1870s when brick became the favoured building material in the village. Elora's riverfront also attracted mills and by 1846 had sixteen enterprises. The most prominent one to survive in stone was a flour mill, known as the Elora Mill, located on the site of the town's first saw mill of 1833. After a fire in 1859 destroyed an 1856 stone structure, owner J. M. Fraser, a fearless and ambitious Scot, immediately hired a team of thirty Scottish stonemasons to rebuild the mill, but again, after a fire in 1866 and another in 1870, it needed at least partial rebuilding. Rising out

the water like a rocky cliff, the Elora Mill formed a massive square block, measuring over eighteen metres on each side, with a run of six millstones. Although J. M. Fraser's empire went bust in 1875 and the mill's riverside wall partially collapsed in 1903, the picturesque mill has proven heroically durable, and in the 1970s was successfully converted into the Elora Mill Inn and Restaurant.

In the 1860s and 1870s, with a population still under two thousand inhabitants, Elora developed a small row of shops on Mill Street West near the mill. The monumental rebuilding of Fraser's stone mill in 1859 may well have been the catalyst. It is not surprising, then,

Above and right: The charming shops on Mill Street West adjacent to the Elora Mill were built of limestone in the 1860s and 1870s. Some have riverside balconies.
Upper right: The Elora Mill, built in 1859 and rebuilt in 1870 after a fire, rises thirty-one metres from base to peak. Its massively thick walls of local limestone were built to withstand flooding and vibrations of the milling equipment.

Top: The Drew House in Elora began as a one-storey stone Regency cottage of the 1850s, then evolved into a two-storey Italianate house during the 1860s, and acquired a Gothic Revival complex on the garden side in the 1870s. Bottom: Due to its rarity, high standard of design, and limestone construction, the 1865 Elora Drill Shed is designated a National Historic Site. This well-proportioned building had many different community uses and now serves as a LCBO store.

to find local limestone used for many of the structures, forming a nucleus of traditional stone rowhouses. In its heyday, these shops provided the basic necessities of life until the 1880s when services and retail shops started migrating up Metcalfe Street to form a new village centre built primarily of brick. After languishing for nearly a century in residential use, Mill Street reinvented itself into an attractive specialty shopping district for arts, crafts, and antiques when the Elora Mill was converted.

Enough wealth was generated in Elora around the mid-century mark that prominent houses began to appear throughout the village, when stone was still the favoured building material. One of the more notable examples is the Drew House, which, on close inspection, shows it was constructed over all three decades, from the 1850s to the 1870s, displaying a parade of architectural fashions under one roof. Stealing the limelight is a three-sided, intricately decorated veranda, which adds a Victorian flair to the mix, while the limestone walls remained suitably subdued in the background. While some of the larger residences were built by merchants and mill owners, the Drew House is named after a lawyer, George Drew, an early settler who bought the one-storey home in the 1860s and expanded it as his star rose and he became the area's first Conservative member of Parliament sent to Ottawa in 1867. As the economy flourished in the late 1860s and early 1870s, successful merchants built substantial new houses. The most exceptional of these houses was Rosemount Cottage, built in the early 1870s for the hardware merchant William Knowles. The stonework is so outstanding that local tradition maintains the unknown mason had worked on the royal castle of Balmoral, Scotland. Rosemount Cottage represents a full-blown example of the Italianate Revival style, a style that gives stonecarvers ample license to excel in their art. With its tall proportions, sculptured architectural features, and garden setting, Rosemount Cottage is a gem of the Italianate movement.

Events outside the small village and even outside British North America have sometimes left a visible trace on the townscape. Fears of Fenian Raids and general concerns generated by the American Civil War led to building more than one hundred drill sheds across the country for training volunteer militia. Elora's is one of only two examples that survive from the original one hundred. Built with funds raised by the community, Elora's 1865 Drill Shed took the form of a permanent and dignified public building built of local limestone in contrast to the more commonly built, cheaper wooden versions. Once the military threat to the border was over by 1870, the drill shed was used continuously as a community centre and Armory Hall. In 1972, it was converted into a most impressive LCBO store, which would no doubt shock those past lecturers of the Temperance Movement who once spoke here.

Even a small village such as Elora joined the province-wide church building movement of the 1870s. Four major churches — Roman Catholic, Anglican, Free Presbyterian, and Knox Presbyterian — were inspired to erect new structures during that decade. All four structures were different, and all are still standing today. Knox Presbyterian Church was built in stone and featured a tall central tower, an ideal form for its location in the centre of Church Square. The agonizing tale of building a beautiful (and expensive) new church in a small place like Elora in the 1870s is well-documented in the *History of Knox Presbyterian Church, Elora, 1837–1987*. Reverend McDonald convinced the Great Western Railway to transport stone from Guelph at half price so they could proceed with construction. The church was completed in 1873 and is still a much loved village landmark.

The stone heritage of Fergus and Elora provides a significant insight into the two communities. To the largely Scottish population of Fergus, stone seemed to be an integral part of the community character and source of civic pride as revealed in its widespread and long-term use as well as in the high quality of craftsmanship found in its durable traditional buildings. Elora's more limited use of stone from the 1850s to the 1870s gives us a glimpse into the brief, but critical turning point when the village came of age as a successful mill settlement in the Grand River valley.

Knox Presbyterian Church was built in 1873 using stone transported from Guelph. The unusually tall, narrow proportions and clean perpendicular line of the centre tower and spire resulted in a delightfully vertical composition.

Guelph

The founding of Guelph in 1827 on the banks of the Speed River had many experiences in common with pioneering settlements along the Grand River. Yet, in a few critical ways, Guelph's experience was different. In the first place, the investors were not individual entrepreneurs, but a well-funded British syndicate called the Canada Company. Their purchase of land, known as the Huron Tract, was the largest in southwestern Upper Canada, over one million acres. The driving force of the Canada Company and its local representative was Scotsman John Galt, a novelist, adventurer, traveller, and idealist with a vision for settling the wilderness of British North America. Whereas most of the fledgling communities simply grew along riverbanks, Galt imposed a fan-shaped plan on Guelph, unlike any other in Upper Canada. Streets radiated out from a central point at the river's edge, enabling easy access to the centre of town from all directions. Furthermore, Galt established public spaces for the most important functions of pioneer community life—the market hall, the Presbyterian and Anglican Churches, and a hilltop site for the Catholic Church—which, although changed, still remain. He named the settlement after the ancestral family of King George I.

During the first year, the Canada Company, as an agency of development, invested heavily in the settlement's earliest needs, providing necessary buildings, roads and bridges, hoping to attract new farmers to the surrounding wilderness. Conditions proved favourable, and the Guelph area eventually developed into a prime agricultural

Left: Wellington Building, built as a hotel in 1877 by local architect Victor Stewart, capitalized on its triangular site with a domed octagonal bay. Its 1980 restoration by architect Karl Briestensky recaptured its spectacular character and promoted the revitalization of downtown Guelph.

The Wellington County Courthouse, built in 1843, was designed in the Gothic Revival style by architect Thomas Young. It is Guelph's oldest existing stone monument and the first to initiate the city's extraordinary commitment to building in locally quarried limestone.

centre. Galt also knew that stone was available locally, for he had ordered two stone quarries to be opened during the first year of settlement. This lovely amber-grey limestone (Guelph dolomite) was strong enough to use as a building material, yet malleable enough to carve into architectural decoration. It could also be converted into an excellent lime mortar, thereby enabling the stone building industry to flourish.

Guelph's propitious beginnings came to fruition several decades later as the settlement matured into a permanent community. From the mid-1850s to the mid-1880s, a new city emerged, created with civic pride and a collective ambition. The first major coup in this evolution occurred even earlier, in 1837, when the Upper Canada government selected Guelph as the District Town for the new Wellington District in a fiercely fought rivalry with Fergus, Galt, and Berlin (now Kitchener). With this designation came the rewards of an administrative centre, government funding, a new jail, and adjacent Wellington County Courthouse. Erected in 1843 to the designs of Thomas Young, an English-trained architect living in Toronto, the new, two-storey courthouse rose up in the midst of this fledgling community of wooden buildings, dominating the surroundings in much the same way a castellated fortress would have done. This battlemented stronghold made it explicitly clear that the colonial government was determined to establish its authority and rule of law over the expanding western settlements.

The next major step in Guelph's coming of age occurred in the euphoric year of 1856: Guelph officially acquired town status, with extensive municipal powers; the Grand Trunk Railroad opened its line from Toronto to downtown Guelph with great fanfare; and the walls of Guelph's magnificent new Town Hall and Market House, now City Hall, were rising. Perhaps it was John Galt's dream for a Royal City that led the town fathers to abandon their modest plans and build one of the finest town halls in the province, costing over ten times the original estimate. William Thomas, Toronto's foremost architect who had a keen interest in sculpture, provided a vigorous rendition of the fashionable Renaissance Revival style. Elaborate stone carvings

Guelph City Hall, built in 1856-1857 by stonemasons Morrison and Emslie to the designs of architect William Thomas, is recognized as a National Historic Site. Guelph limestone is suitable for decorative purposes.

Medical Hall, built in 1858–1859 as an apothecary for Nathaniel Higinbotham, shows the high-quality masonry that characterized the early years of the limestone movement. Owners since 1919, the Toronto-Dominion Bank restored the building for Guelph's sesquicentennial in 1977.

maximized the effect of all arched openings. Corner quoins, brackets, and pilasters further animated the façade. This was the ultimate achievement in architectural sculpture brought about by the fortuitous union of a talented architect-sculptor, high-quality limestone, and skilled stonecarvers.

The building of the Grand Trunk Railway in 1853–1856 had brought masons to Guelph to build the massive stone railway viaducts and retaining walls. By 1861, when the population of the town was only 5,076, the residents included 56 stonemasons: 28 English; 18 Scottish; and 10 other, most of them trained in Britain. The railway boom meant prosperity, construction, and regular employment for masons. The local stone quarries continued to provide an unlimited supply of good building stone and lime. These factors conspired to launch Guelph into a golden age of stone buildings. In an amazingly unified approach, leaders in every facet of community life—government, religious, commercial, and industrial—as well as many homeowners built structures using the local limestone.

After the railroad cut through Market Square, isolating the earliest commercial area, the present-day core formed around the new Town Hall and Market House, starting in the 1850s along lower Wyndham Street with the building of three-storey stone commercial rows. Representative buildings from three decades show how the development progressed. Medical Hall, built in 1858–1859, illustrates the superb quality of local limestone construction in the early years, when the walls were built of smooth, tightly fitted ashlar blocks, and the windows were encased in carved stone surrounds with sculptured lintels. The Alma Block, built in 1867 further up Wyndham Street, shows the continuation of this tradition, but with the variations of arched windows and delightfully floating, straight and curved lintels. The Wellington Building, built in 1876–1877 at the corner of Upper Wyndham and Woolwich Streets, introduced the highly fashionable Second Empire style to the streetscape, emphasizing the entrance to the commercial core by its domed octagonal corner bay.

Guelph prospered throughout the 1860s and 1870s, more than doubling its population, and acquiring city status (a population of

10,000 was a prerequisite) in 1879 when it officially became known as the Royal City. With its municipal powers, the city could offer incentives to new business, and industries increased as steam power became available. The new rail lines enabled the movement of Guelph's products. This general prosperity is recorded on Wyndham Street where two- and three-storey commercial blocks formed a continuous streetscape by 1885. Despite the rich variety of architectural styles, buildings consistently utilized the same Guelph limestone, a consistent set-back, and often a continuous cornice line. Taken together, this collective effort created an extraordinarily harmonious downtown of stone. Stone buildings on the side streets reinforced the character of downtown, but it was in the city's heart of St. George's Square where exuberant High Victorian stone monuments reached a crescendo (all unfortunately since replaced). Even with these changes, Guelph's limestone downtown ranks among the finest in the province.

Alma Block, built in 1867 and designed by Toronto architect James Smith, contributes significantly to the architectural interest of Wyndham Street, where buildings were built in long rows and displayed a wealth of carved stone detail.

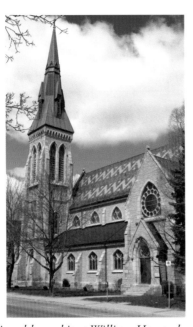

Left: St. Andrew's Presbyterian Church, designed by architect William Hay and built in 1857–1858, was the first Gothic Revival church in Guelph. Masons Morrison and Elmslie, the builders of the Town Hall the year before, continued their high standard of masonry in the closely fitted ashlar limestone.

Right: St. George's Anglican Church, built in 1873 to the designs of architect Henry Langley of Toronto, illustrates a later version of the Gothic Revival style. Masons were now using rough textural surfaces popular in the 1870s in contrast to the earlier smooth ashlar block.

More than in the other stone towns of southwestern Ontario, Guelph's passion for building in local stone found expression in the flowering of its church architecture, reflecting the dominant role religion played in the nineteenth century. Eleven of the twelve stone churches were built in local limestone between 1856 and 1891 (the one exception was Chalmers Presbyterian Church, a limestone building with a granite fieldstone façade). Most were integrated into the urban fabric and all were products of considerable civic pride mixed, no doubt, with a healthy dose of religious rivalry. It is extraordinary that so many of these Guelph denominations hired Toronto's leading church architects to prepare designs—Henry Langley, James Smith, R. C. Windeyer, and Joseph Connolly. Almost all these churches were designed in the popular Gothic Revival style. Three examples have been selected, each representative of its decade. The earliest and one of the finest was St. Andrew's Presbyterian Church, built in 1857–1858 and designed by Scottish architect William Hay of Toronto and assisted by David Allan of Guelph. Although the Presbyterians had sold their pre-eminent site to the town for its new Town Hall in 1856, they compensated by erecting a dramatically assertive stone edifice several blocks away. Its central tower and forty-six-metre-high spire made it a landmark on the surrounding townscape. All energy seemed to be concentrated in the verticality of design, all features subordinated to the tall tower and prominent stepped buttresses.

In 1873, St. George's Anglican Church, as had St. Andrew's two decades earlier, abandoned its original premiere site assigned by John Galt in the centre of St. George's Square (which had already caused traffic problems!), and erected a Gothic Revival structure in a scenic location by the river. The new church captured the essence of the style as it came to fruition in the 1870s. In the hands of the province's most proficient church architect of the time, Henry Langley, St. George's embraces the most fashionable Victorian ideals: the soaring verticality of its corner tower; the absolute clarity of architectural expression; and the Victorian yearning for the picturesque in its riverside setting.

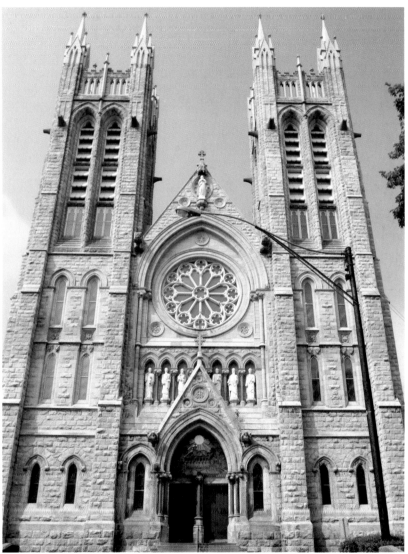

The crowning glory of Guelph churches, however, is the splendid Church of Our Lady of the Immaculate Conception, 1876–1888, a Roman Catholic edifice that reigns serenely over the city. Its sixty-one-metre-high twin towers, added later in 1926, dominate the skyline. How awe-inspiring it must have been to see a thirteenth-century European cathedral materialize on "Catholic Hill" in the 1880s. This structure, the third church to be built on the site, is the masterpiece of church architect Joseph Connolly, who was familiar with the great cathedrals of his native Ireland. Building a "medieval cathedral" in North America in the nineteenth century was unusual; in Ontario, it was especially rare. In true cathedral form, the nave became articulated with triforium and clerestory levels, side aisles and transept, and an ambulatory and seven radiating chapels around the apse. Stonework, typical of the 1880s, was quarry-faced and coursed. Its rugged texture provided an animated surface that needed little additional sculpture,

Our Lady of the Immaculate Conception was designed by architect Joseph Connolly and built in 1876–1888. Its distinctive twin towers were added in 1926.

Upper right: The Perry-Scroggie House is Guelph's only five-bay Ontario Cottage.
Top: The modest McTague Cottages are embellished with carved architectural ornament.
Botton: The McCrae Birthplace Museum was built ca. 1858 with a 1860s addition. Poet John McCrae, author of "In Flanders Fields," was born here in 1872.

unlike its predecessors of the Middle Ages. This is the one church that retained its original location assigned by John Galt in 1827, and one whose magnificence perhaps even exceeded Galt's highest expectations.

Enthusiasm for building in stone was not confined to public and prominent buildings alone. Stone was also used with pride by homeowners whether for their modest cottages or palatial villas. The prosperity and accompanying building spree witnessed in the commercial and public sphere carried over in full force into domestic architecture. In the 1850s, stone houses of all shapes and sizes first started appearing in and around the downtown. The more modest examples clustered either near the river or outside the core; the grandest homes occupied prime real estate along the hilltops; and the largely middle-class houses filled in the streets on the rising terraces along the river. These stone houses reveal much about Guelph's settlement pattern of the mid-to-late nineteenth century.

The ever-popular, vernacular dwelling called the Ontario Cottage—the standard one-storey home with hip roof, overhanging eaves, end chimneys, and central doorway—was common in Guelph and often served as the home of craftsmen and skilled workers. One of the most distinguished is the Perry-Scroggie House, built in 1854–1855, whose first occupant, Thomas Day, a stonemason from Yorkshire, was possibly the builder of the house. Here, the generously large, shuttered windows have usurped the front façade, "squeezing" the front doorway into narrow sidelights. Another, simpler, example is the McCrae Birthplace Museum. It was built in ca. 1858 and acquired a sizable wing in the 1860s. It is now famous as the birthplace in 1872 of soldier-physician-poet John McCrae, author of the First World War poem, "In Flanders Fields." Under threat of demolition to make way for a new high-rise apartment building, the homestead was saved in the nick of time by an action group formed in 1966. That same year John McCrae was declared a person of National Historic Significance and his birthplace a National Historic Site. An aspect of the Ontario Cottage style that is specific to Guelph occurs in the richly decorated versions that boast beautiful stone sculptures over windows and doorway. The McTague Cottages, built ca.1865–1870s, represent a rare cluster of four decorated cottages, each one with its own form of ornamentation.

One of the outstanding specialists in this architectural art form was Matthew Bell, a stonecarver from Newcastle, England, who owned a quarry in Guelph and worked from the 1850s until his death in 1883. He left a legacy of beautiful stone carving throughout the city. Bell built three houses in Guelph for his family of ten children—each one different, yet each one a masterwork of exterior sculpture as well as a unique expression of his own personal whimsy. In his second house, the House of Heads, built in 1858, Bell introduced his talent for figurative sculpture in the eight animated portraits on the front façade (still unidentified). As this house was built shortly after architect-sculptor William Thomas erected the new Town Hall and Market House, it is speculated that Thomas could have inspired Bell to pursue this art form to new heights. In the third Matthew Bell House, built in 1867–1872, he concentrated primarily on the elegantly sculptured architectural trim that was in vogue with the Italianate Revival style. This time he limited his figurative sculpture to three portraits on the central bay, including the bust of a man

The 1858 House of Heads was stonecarver Matthew Bell's second home.

Above and right: The Matthew Bell House, his third house, was built in 1867–1872. The home illustrates his progression into robust architectural ornamentation in the elegantly carved window surrounds, arched and pedimented lintels, and segmental pilasters. Three portraits look out from the centre bay.
Upper and lower right: Woolwich Street, built 1864–1865, demonstrates how carved architectural ornamentation could enhance a traditional façade. The stonework is attributed to Matthew Bell.

Ker Cavan, built ca. 1857, represents one of Guelph's earliest country estates. This grand Elizabethan residence stood high on the north hill overlooking the town, appearing more like a bishop's palace than Rev. Palmer's parsonage.

thought to be Charles Dickens, his favourite author. A larger house at 264 Woolwich Street, built in 1864–1865, is attributed to Matthew Bell based on the exterior's significant carved architectural trim. Under his hand, Bell could imbue a rather traditional dwelling with a sense of monumentality, transforming it into a far grander residence. Each architectural feature, whether window, door, corner, or projecting bay, is given special three-dimensional treatment with lintels, arches, quoins, and brackets. This type of stonework was a specialty of Guelph.

The city also had its share of wealthy entrepreneurs who developed impressive estates in the manner of the British country gentleman. The earliest and rather unexpected "developer" of a country villa was the

Wyoming, begun in 1866, was completed in 1885 by J. W. Lyon, Guelph's first millionaire. This high-styled villa was built in the Second Empire style on the north hill among other fashionable estates. The present owners have restored the mansion to its former glory.

Anglican rector, Reverend Arthur Palmer, an ambitious young man from Ireland with grand ideas and a good business sense. Around 1857, he built his parsonage (in fact, a grand estate) Ker Cavan (originally known as Tyrcathlen), which has been rumoured to be the work of Sir Charles Barry, architect of the Parliament Buildings in London. Although unconfirmed, it must be acknowledged that the residence was the work of a superior architect, fully versed in the Elizabethan-inspired Gothic Revival style. Skilled masons constructed the premises in dressed ashlar limestone. Nearby on the same north hill stands another great mansion, Wyoming, that grew up from a one-storey stone house built in 1866 into a full-blown Second Empire style mansion by 1885, designed by local architect John Hall Jr. As Guelph's most exuberant High Victorian residence, it possesses a profusion of ornamentation that culminates in the central four-storey, mansard-roofed tower.

Stone was indigenous to Guelph; the city was built of it and upon it. It was easily procured at a reasonable price so that all kinds of buildings could be built with it. From the 1850s to the 1880s, Guelph evolved into a city of stone, renowned for its superior limestone, high-quality masonry work, and distinctive carved ornamentation. In 1951, Guelph still retained 870 stone buildings, considerably more than any other place in southwestern Ontario. No wonder that local limestone has become an integral part of Guelph's sense of place.

Region of Waterloo

As the Grand River wends its way southward from Fergus and Elora, it passes through the sandy loam plain of the Waterloo region. It is an area where the soil was so favourable for farming that when it first became available in 1800, a group of Mennonites from Pennsylvania formed the General Company and began procuring a vast tract of land. Their intention was to resettle their community, coming first to Waterloo Township (so named in 1816) and then later to Woolwich and Wilmot Townships. Their original imprint on the beautiful rolling landscape is visible today; their farmhouses, bank barns, and farmlands, although reduced in size, still exist. From their years in Pennsylvania, these Mennonite settlers were experienced farmers and familiar with the local tradition of building in fieldstone. Fieldstone was abundantly available in the Waterloo region, scattered throughout the landscape by the retreating glaciers. After the farmers had cleared their fields, the stones lay piled in mounds and along the fence lines, awaiting more propitious times. The story of stone buildings in the Waterloo region is primarily the story of Mennonite farmhouses, beautiful in their simplicity, stalwart and yet graceful in the way they belong to the landscape. Recognizably distinct, these farmhouses are a specialty of the rural Waterloo region.

Stone towns did not develop along this winding section of the Grand River as they had farther north in Fergus and Elora. Glacial debris had buried the limestone bedrock so deep that stone quarrying was not possible. Nor did stone buildings appear in any numbers in

Left: Swope House, built ca. 1858 in West Montrose, is a fine example of the fieldstone Mennonite farmhouse. The two-storey veranda with Victorian trim offers a beautiful view over the Grand River valley, but interestingly its main front door is not accessible from the outside.

the urban areas of Berlin (now Kitchener) and Waterloo. Further south, however, in the Galt (now Cambridge) area, another major stone centre took hold, but that is a story for the next chapter.

Of German-Swiss-Dutch ancestry, the Mennonites had fled to Pennsylvania in the eighteenth century, bringing their language and traditions with them. In terms of their religion and cultural heritage, they were a relatively homogeneous group, speaking a Pennsylvania-German dialect in preference to English. With their shared values of self-sufficiency and a cooperative work ethic, they had acquired capital and personal goods that they brought with them in their Conestoga wagons—quite a different experience from the fleeing United Empire Loyalists who had lost everything or the European immigrants who had travelled by sea. They were the first major group to immigrate into the far interior of Upper Canada, which only a few years earlier had belonged to the Six Nations Confederacy. Land was inexpensive, and they were one to three decades ahead of British settlements in the area.

As a group, the Mennonites bought a vast tract of land (part of Block 2) together and subsequently drew lots for assigning each family to a farm. They had paid cash up front, which allowed them to divide and develop their lands as they chose. For example, in 1805, the German Company, formed by a group of 26 individuals from Lancaster County, Pennsylvania, bought 60,000 acres of what is now Waterloo Township along the Grand River for £10,795. Farms were often large (in 1831, the average holding by a pioneer from Lancaster County was 355 acres).

Although immigration was temporarily interrupted by the War of 1812, new settlers kept coming from Pennsylvania, increasing the population to 1,825 by 1827. By 1831, these pioneers owned eighty-seven percent of the assessed land in Waterloo Township. Reports of a thriving settlement reached back home. One settler wrote back to his family in Lancaster County in 1819: "if you perchance have in mind moving to this country, I would consider it the sooner the better, for it is being settled fast. I think the price of land will rise considerably, although at present one can still choose what one wishes. There is rapid buying and selling, and people are very active in building and clearing."

It was in the 1830s and 1840s when their farms were beginning to flourish that the Mennonites started building finer replacement houses of stone. Free and already on site, fieldstone became the prized building material for the next two decades. The David Weber House, built ca. 1840s, represents the simplest form of the new stone houses—one-and-a-half storeys high with walls of uncoursed, split fieldstone of various sizes and colours, set in liberal amounts of mortar, typical of Mennonite masonry. Characteristic also was the front veranda with a plastered wall behind. David Weber, having arrived from Pennsylvania in 1807, farmed this land and raised fifteen children under this roof as well as holding Mennonite religious services here, until a meeting house was erected across the street in 1843.

The Mennonites were able to bring with them not only enough capital to hire farm labour, but also a stock of seeds and tools as well as proven farming methods. They set a high standard of farming in these pioneer years: Adam Fergusson (the founder of Fergus) observed

David Weber House in Kitchener, built ca. 1840s, typifies the early stone farmhouses built by Mennonites in Waterloo Township. In 1981, the home barely survived demolition during suburban redevelopment. New owners restored the exterior and rare early stencilling on the interior.

in his travels of 1831 in North America that the typical Mennonite farm contained "from 200 to 300 acres, laid out in regular fields, and not a stump to be seen. The ploughing was capital, the crops most luxuriant, and the cattle, horses etc. of a superior stamp, with handsome houses, barns etc. and orchards promising rich returns. Waterloo satisfied me above all that I had yet seen of the capability of Canada to become a fruitful and fine country."

By comparison, the Adam Ferrie Jr. House built ca. 1840 in nearby Doon (now part of Kitchener), is characteristically Scottish. Located on the Old Huron Road, the house stands on land bought from the Mennonites in 1834. Son of the Honourable Adam Ferrie Sr. of Montreal, a wealthy entrepreneur and politician, Adam Jr. was the founder of Doon Mills on Schneider's Creek, where he built a sawmill (now a ruin, often painted by artist Homer Watson), flour, barley, and oat mills, as well as a distillery by 1839. In contrast to the random-sized, patchwork look of Mennonite masonry, the stonework of the Ferrie house displays a front façade of limestone that was uniform in height, a consistent grey colour, and laid in narrow courses. The front windows, measuring 1.4 metres by 2.7 metres with twenty-four window panes, are extraordinarily large for its early date.

By 1850, the original Mennonite pioneers and their descendants were becoming increasingly prosperous and could finally afford to hire stonemasons to build more substantial farmsteads. The Woolner House, built ca. 1857, clearly demonstrates Mennonite minister-and-farmer Abraham Weber's decision to build a fine, two-storey stone house after outgrowing the first, smaller stone dwelling of the 1830s (now the kitchen wing). They continued the Mennonite traditions of building in uncoursed fieldstone and adding the characteristic veranda with plastered wall behind (at the rear), and two small square attic

Adam Ferrie Jr. House in Kitchener, built ca. 1840, illustrates the contrast of masonry between a Scottish home with its coursed, matching grey stones and the Mennonite random-sized fieldstone construction that was heavily mortared.

Woolner House in Kitchener, built in ca. 1857, is a fieldstone Mennonite farmhouse that still occupies a scenic rural location by the Grand River. The Woolner family has owned the property since 1908.

windows in the end gables. The Woolner family, who purchased the property nearly a century ago, has carefully preserved the home, bank barn (ca. 1870s), and six acres of scenic lands along the Grand River.

The Mennonite settlers were rural by preference and had little need of establishing towns, beyond the necessary mills, blacksmith shops, and meeting houses. Because no road allowances were laid out between lots, farmers often followed the contours of the land or travelled through the poorest sections of their farms. Even today, the Waterloo region reflects this original settlement pattern of extensive farmlands, scattered hamlets, and an informal road system.

By 1861 forty-six two-storey stone farmhouses had been built in Waterloo Township alone. This included the Brubacher House, built in 1850. Son of "1816 John" (so named for the year he arrived from Lancaster County), John E. Brubacher established his homestead on a 254-acre farm north of the community of Waterloo on land that is now part of the University of Waterloo campus. There he raised fifteen

children and farmed for the rest of the century. The house, still surrounded by open grounds, is a quintessential Mennonite farmhouse, open as a museum at specified times. Built of uncoursed, multi-coloured fieldstone, it has a full veranda on the garden side with its traditional plastered wall behind. The attic, where traditionally meat was cured, had the characteristic small, square windows in the gable ends.

Situated north and east of Kitchener-Waterloo is Woolwich Township where the Grand River meanders its way southwards through a rural landscape. It was into this area that the Mennonite farmers expanded once the land in Waterloo Township had been taken up. Although the German Company had purchased 45,000 acres in Woolwich Township as early as 1816, settlement had been more gradual—the Mennonite communities of St. Jacobs and Elmira were not founded until 1830 and 1840, respectively. In the Woolwich area today, a number of stone farmhouses are still occupied by Mennonites, ranging from the strictest Old Order, who ban the use of electricity and motor vehicles, to the new orders, who accept modern practices. One of the finest Mennonite houses in Woolwich Township is the Swope House, built ca.1858. Situated on a hillside with its gable end to the street, the house has a two-storey front veranda of Victorian detail that overlooks the scenic Grand River valley of West Montrose, a hamlet well-known for its picturesque covered bridge. Carefully restored by the present owners, the house displays the elegant simplicity of line and beauty of material characteristic of Mennonite stone farmhouses. Typical features include mixed fieldstone construction, plastered walls of the veranda, and small, square, attic windows.

Not all stone buildings in the area were Mennonite farmhouses— some were schools and churches in the outlying places. The West Montrose Schoolhouse, built in 1874 by stonemason Fred Struck on a rising slope across the river, has a charming, five-bay façade, arched

Brubacher House, built in 1850 and restored in 1975, is now a Mennonite house museum on the University of Waterloo campus. Typically, the house is asymmetrical and the front door opens directly into the kitchen.

openings, and an abundantly mortared fieldstone construction. When the school closed in 1966, its domestic appearance made it a natural candidate for conversion into a private dwelling. The landscaped setting, central fanlight doorway, and spacious interior dimensions are ideal for its new use as a residence.

The Mennonite and Amish community also expanded westward from Waterloo Township in the 1820s when several members reserved the newly opened Crown Reserve lands for the County of Lincoln, now Wilmot Township (owned in part by King's College, later the University of Toronto). They acted on behalf of closely related Amish

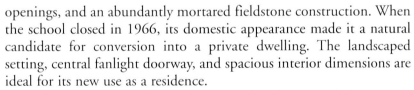

Above and right: Swope House front and back views.
Lower right: West Montrose Schoolhouse, built in 1874, functioned as a schoolhouse until 1966 when this charming building was converted into a residence. It demonstrates that in the Waterloo area, occasionally public buildings were constructed of fieldstone in the small hamlets.

Joseph Zehr House, built in 1857 in Baden, is part of an original Mennonite complex of farm buildings. The squared and coursed fieldstone of the German Block differs somewhat from the random-coursed fieldstone construction found in Waterloo and Woolwich Townships.

immigrants from Alsace, the Palatinate, and Wüttemberg, who established what is known as the "German Block." Once settled in the Wilmot area, the Amish and Mennonite farmers began building stone houses in the 1850s and 1860s. As a group, the houses show quite a variety, but in contrast to their more eastern neighbours, they tended to be more formal, symmetrical, and with a higher quality of masonry, perhaps due to European influence. A rare case where a family has retained ownership of a homestead since it was built in 1857 is the Joseph Zehr House in Baden. The large fieldstone blocks on the façade indicate skilled masonry work. Five generations of the Wagler family, direct descendents of Joseph Zehr, have farmed the land and maintained the original buildings, an extraordinary collection that features the main stone house, a stone cottage, a bank barn, a cheese and meat house, and a pumphouse.

The records of the Moses Hostetler House, built in 1860 near New Hamburg, indicate that the stonemason was Hyacinth Roth who had emigrated from Germany to undertake this construction project. A skilled craftsman, Roth built one of the finest stone houses in the area, utilizing split fieldstone that he cut into blocks, matched in size, and laid in courses. He also incorporated smooth limestone for lintels and corner quoins, and on the front façade placed a date stone—"M.&.M. H.1860"—for Mary and Moses Hostetler. Stylistically, this farmhouse, with its Doric columned porch, signalled a move to the more popular Classical Revival style and away from the traditional Mennonite form, indicating perhaps the beginning of assimilation into their new culture.

These stone farmhouses, as representatives of a much larger collection of Mennonite stone farmhouses in the Waterloo area, show how remarkably well they have retained their authentic historical character— most have retained their rural setting and some are still lived in by Mennonite farmers. As a close-knit community dedicated to a traditional way of life, Mennonites have a commitment to their cultural heritage that is unrivalled. Their homesteads, built solidly and maintained well, take us directly back to pioneer times more than 150 years ago, when the Waterloo region was the exemplary "fruitful and fine country" and the promise of Canada to come.

The Moses Hostetler House was built in 1860 in New Hamburg by the German stonemason, Hyacinth Roth. The walls of squared field granite, uniform in size and laid in courses, reveal the superb craftsmanship of the masonry.

Cambridge

As the Grand River meanders southward from the Waterloo area, it meets up with its tributary, the Speed River, at Preston. Over the millennia, both the Speed and the Grand carved their way through the area's stony landscape, exposing a fine dolomite similar to the building stone found in Guelph. While this quarried limestone supplied the villages of Hespeler, Preston, Blair, and Galt by the 1850s, surprisingly, it was another stone that transformed the image of Galt. Known as the granite city, Galt will be the focus of this chapter, although all four of these communities, amalgamated into Cambridge in 1979, have a heritage of notable stone buildings. In contrast to its neighbouring German communities, Galt was a Scottish settlement. Its well-trained masons found a different but familiar stone to work with—granite, a hard stone found in the Canadian Shield that glaciers had moved southwards in chunks and abandoned on the landscape in their retreat. Granite was never quarried locally, but split from fieldstones and boulders found commonly on the area's farmlands.

In 1816, the Honourable William Dickson, born in Dumfries, Scotland, and then a legislative councillor and prominent attorney living in Niagara, purchased 94,305 acres of unbroken forest along the Grand River (at about $1.00 per acre). Perhaps it was his earlier work as a lawyer for the Mennonites during their purchase of Waterloo Township that led him to speculate on this massive land purchase of Block 1 of the Six Nations Confederacy territory. He hired as his agent a young carpenter from Pennsylvania, Absalom Shade, and together

Former Galt Post Office was built in 1885 by the federal government using local variegated fieldstone. Designed by Chief Architect Thomas Fuller, this showpiece of stone construction brought the exuberance of the High Victorian style to downtown Galt.

they trekked through the dense bush along the Grand until arriving at the point where Mill Creek joined the river. Here, a beautiful oval valley opened up with high ridges on either side. With its ample supply of water power, the site proved ideal for a new settlement. Immediately Absalom Shade procured the machinery for a mill from New York state and established grist and saw mills and a store, calling it Shade's Mills.

Dickson kept in close contact with his homeland, urging fellow Scots through articles in the press or by personal letter to immigrate to his new settlement. He also sent his own representative to Scotland to generate business. When John Galt, an old Edinburgh school friend, arrived in 1827 to establish Guelph, Dickson heartily supported his endeavours. Galt agreed to build a twenty-six kilometre road (Highway 24) connecting the two communities. That same year, Dickson named his own settlement in Galt's honour. A sense of kinship made immigration considerably more appealing; by the 1830s the township was composed largely of educated, hard-working Scots, and the common saying was "None but the Lowland Scotchmen would ever have cleared North Dumfries." Although the German settlement of Preston was only five kilometres away, Dickson's settlement seems to have developed quite separately.

Dickson's sons likewise contributed to furthering the growth of Galt. William Jr. settled permanently in Galt on the west ridge of town known as Dickson Hill where he built Kirkmichael in 1832, considered one of the province's outstanding Regency cottages. Built of random-coursed limestone with a semi-elliptical fanlight door, this elegant Ontario Cottage is a rare inland example of a style found more commonly in the early settlements along the lakeshore. In fact, it was not unlike a house his father owned in Niagara that had been burned by the retreating American soldiers in 1813. In 1837, the oldest son, Robert, hired an engineer from Montreal to build a dam and canal at

Left: Kirkmichael was built in 1832 for William Dickson Jr.
Upper left: Dickson Mill was built as a grist mill in 1843 for William's brother, Robert. It is Galt's oldest stone industrial building.

Park Hill Road where Robert erected his Dickson Mill in 1843. As Galt's oldest surviving industrial building, the mill bears witness to the solidity of this early limestone construction, withstanding seasonal and sometimes disastrous flooding of the Grand River. Dickson's dam and canal attracted other water-powered industries to locate nearby. With Robert's working grist mill, farmers could bring their produce in for milling and then haul it down the newly (1837) macadamized Dundas-Waterloo Road for export through the Desjardins Canal (opened 1837). Galt was becoming the best grain market for thirty-to-forty kilometres around, and the community was beginning to flourish. Interwoven into pioneer community life were the founding and growth of religious groups—Presbyterians were the leaders (sixty percent of Galt residents were Presbyterians in 1851), but the split caused by the Dissension of 1843 in Scotland resulted in several factions erecting separate churches, all of them later replaced. The Anglicans, although greatly in the minority, benefited from the substantial donations of founders William Dickson and Absalom Shade toward building the lovely Gothic Revival sanctuary of Trinity Anglican Church. Built in 1844, Trinity Church was constructed of locally quarried limestone, as were the other pre-1850s stone buildings. Over the years it was enlarged and in 1885 acquired the traditional Norman tower designed by Toronto architect R. C. Windeyer. Situated on the Grand River and facing Trinity Park, this peaceful enclave provides a rare glimpse into Galt's formative years.

Typical of many communities in southwestern Ontario, Galt entered a new era in the 1850s. It became incorporated as a village in 1850 and as a town in 1857; a branch of the Great Western Railway (GWR) was completed in 1855 linking the GWR with the Grand Trunk Railway at Guelph in 1857; and its abundant water power hastened industrial growth with the development of foundries and factories. Interestingly, when the time came to build the Town Hall, now City Hall, in 1858, local architect H. B. Sinclair conceived a Classical version that was both spirited and innovative. It boasted a fashionable Italianate entrance tower—a design said to be found in the

Trinity Anglican Church, begun in 1844 (sanctuary), is considered to be the oldest stone church in Waterloo County. Built of limestone in the Gothic Revival style, it was enlarged over the years into an attractive complex.

The former Galt Town Hall was built in 1858 to the designs of local architect H.B. Sinclair. The use of matching grey granite walls with limestone trim marked the beginning of a trend that led Galt to be known as the Granite City.

Scottish Lowlands—and a new building material—granite—a stone well-known to Scottish masons. In the hands of an experienced craftsman, this hard, crystalline rock could be split into squared, rough-faced blocks with skillfully directed hammer blows. Amazingly, the granite in the Galt Town Hall was cut from field boulders, then squared, matched in both size and in colour (as if cut from a single quarry), and laid in courses on all four sides. Granite construction had already appeared by the early 1850s, but these earlier examples are recognized by their use of multi-coloured stones. As the community's first major structure using matched grey granite, the Town Hall inaugurated a specialized local trend, one that lasted only a few decades, but one that still characterizes the city today.

Industrial prosperity of the mills and foundries continued to attract more people and more business so that by the 1850s, Galt's Main Street from Ainslie to Water Streets began transforming itself from a random

collection of frame structures into a cohesive streetscape of noble stone buildings that have remained largely intact. By 1866, Galt claimed the pre-eminent economic position in Waterloo County, and it showed in the new image of Main Street: "nowhere in Waterloo County was local stone used so impressively, and so extensively, as in the business blocks of nineteenth-century Galt." In this era, builders still had an innate sense of visual relationships, ensuring that structures had an almost continuous cornice line and façades were of matched, squared granite. Collectively, the business people of Galt were creating a harmonious, uniform business core of granite just as the merchants of Guelph were doing in limestone.

By the 1850s and 1860s, stone became the building material of choice for all types of buildings, particularly houses—the Census of 1891 recorded that Galt had acquired 338 stone dwellings. As in Guelph and Fergus, the one-storey Ontario Cottage was a great favourite of the craftsmen. Many of these cottages were located close to the river, such as the McDougall Cottage built ca. 1858 for John McDougall who worked as a carpenter across the street at Dumfries Foundry (now Southworks). Even in this modest Ontario Cottage, the

Upper left: McDougall Cottage, a granite and limestone Ontario Cottage, built in 1858 for Scotsman John McDougall, is now a museum open to the public. Rare wall and ceiling paintings decorate the interior.

Top: Main Street-North Side, the grey granite and traditional format of these 1860s and 1870s commercial buildings provide continuity in Galt's business district.

Bottom: Goldie and McCulloch (later Babcock & Wilcox) was built originally as Dumfries Foundry in 1847 and subsequently enlarged.

Far right: Thornhill, built of fieldstone in the late 1850s, was the residence of the Honourable John Young, a well-known politician who served in all levels of government and authored many books, including his reminiscences of early Galt, written under this roof.

Above and right: The Cedars was built initially in 1855, and then twenty years later enlarged into a stately mansion of Italianate Revival Style. The carved limestone of the arched windows shows an exceptionally high level of craftsmanship.

stone used on the primary street façade was the now-fashionable, coursed, grey granite with limestone trim, although the remaining façades were built of fieldstone. A number of early stone houses, one and two-storeys high, still dot the downtown streets on both sides of the river, interwoven into the commercial fabric of the present-day city. Those built later can also be found interspersed throughout the residential neighbourhoods on the hills. The grandest stone homes often occupied prime sites on the edge of the bluffs. Thornhill, built in the late 1850s, represents the classic, well-proportioned, fashionable Italianate residence with a lovely full veranda on its downhill side (the original front façade), offering a stunning view westward over the city and river valley. It was the home of the Honourable James Young (1835–1915), one of Galt's most distinguished politicians, for many years. Across the river on the brow of Dickson Hill, a corresponding Italianate residence

Left: Galt Foundry and Machine Works (later Canada Machinery Corporation) built of limestone ca. 1875, demonstrates the pride of craftsmanship the early stonemasons had. The pleasing scale and proportions of the façade suggest an extended rowhouse terrace. Below: Glen Echo, a farmhouse built in 1857, combines granite walls with a lively pattern of limestone quoins edging the windows, doorway, and corners. Dumfries masons liked to use the "peacock-fan" voussoirs in the gable and occasionally placed a chimney up through it.

looks back eastward over the city and valley. Known as the Cedars, this mansion may have first been built as a one-storey limestone cottage in 1855 and then enlarged in the early 1870s into a one-of-a-kind, ornate, Italianate showpiece. The smooth refined lines of the window arches represent some of the most elaborate stone sculpture in Galt, a sharp contrast to the prevailing rough-faced granite. The Cedars' main façade also faces downhill. Its large proportions, projecting frontispiece, and classical porch impart a stately appearance. By contrast, many of the less-elaborate houses were delightfully charming in their vernacular use of patterned stone. Glen Echo, built in 1857 as a farmhouse (now surrounded by a housing development), shows how animated a façade can be with the interplay between light limestone quoins and darker granite walls. The peacock-fan design of the tapered voussoirs in the gable ("gothick") window was a favourite detail of the Scottish masons in Dumfries Township.

As Galt moved into the 1870s and 1880s, the driving force for the town's prosperity was its expanding manufacturing sector, fuelled by both water and steam power. The arrival of the railway opened new markets not only in southern Ontario but also in the western Canada and northeastern United States. Galt had developed a strong base of grain and woollen mills as well as numerous metal foundries that, in turn, attracted related industries. In 1866, Galt was listed as having over $1,000,000 invested in capital. By 1881, the value of its products was reported at over $2,000,000, duly earning its reputation as the "Manchester of Canada." In 1859, Goldie and McCulloch, Founders, Engineers and Machinists, now the Southworks Outlet Mall, bought the small Dumfries Foundry of 1847 and expanded it into a large-scale supplier of engines, boilers, water wheels, mill machinery, safes, and wool-processing machinery—a complete mill outfitter. These two- and three-storey rubblestone structures, impressive for their sheer magnitude and massive stonework, comprise a two-acre complex dating from the mid- to late-nineteenth century. Across the river on the east side, the premises of the limestone Galt Foundry and Machine Works, built in 1875, likewise testify to a bygone industrial era, when stonemasons built on a huge scale (in this case, twenty-three bays long), but still employed a high standard of craftsmanship, giving special attention to the corner detailing.

Also reflected in Galt's stone architecture was the townspeople's ambition for the town to be not only an industrial centre, but also a place both beautiful and cosmopolitan. This is no better illustrated than in the two high-styled Gothic Revival churches sited near the river—Knox Presbyterian Church and Central Presbyterian Church—each with a tall spire announcing its presence on the lovely open space of Queen's Square. The two together—one the counterpoint to the other—tell us how important religion was to the founding Scottish families and even how important the divisions within the Presbyterian Church were, following the Dissension of 1843 in Scotland. Knox Church, erected in 1868–1870 to the plans of Toronto architect James Smith, featured

Left and above: Knox Presbyterian Church, designed by architect James Smith and built in 1868–1870, was the first of the two Presbyterian churches to locate on Queen's Square. This commanding edifice is an affirmation of the congregation's break with the established church.

Preceding page: Central Presbyterian Church, built in 1880–1882 and designed by architects Hall and Mallory, restored the balance on Queen's Square with an equally affirming presence. Both Presbyterian churches are Gothic Revival in style and constructed of granite with limestone trim.

Dickson Public School, built in 1876–1877, is Galt's one surviving nineteenth-century public school built of coursed limestone. The building sits firmly on the brow of Dickson Hill and is a neighbourhood landmark.

the combined use of granite and limestone with a dominating central tower that was heavily buttressed and surmounted by an octagonal wooden spire. Across the square, Central Church, built later, in 1880–1882, to the designs of architects Hall and Mallory of Toronto, also used granite and limestone construction, but with a side tower, slender tall spire, and large, traceried windows in the gable façades.

After the third-quarter mark of the nineteenth century, the use of stone construction was beginning to decline, yet local stone was still favoured for major public buildings. Galt was well-known for its stone schools, the most famous one—Galt Collegiate Institute—

which despite its Victorian appearance acquired its Scottish baronial appearance in the twentieth century and, therefore, is not included here. Representative of the nineteenth-century group is the Dickson Public School, designed by William Scott and built in 1876–1877 in coursed limestone by mason William Webster. This handsome building with bracketed eaves, projecting pedimented bays, and a bellcote on the roof stands on the height of Dickson Hill, very much as solid and appealing as when it was first built. Not only did the municipal government build in stone, but so did the federal government when they erected the former Galt Post Office in 1885. Designed by Canada's Chief Architect, Thomas Fuller, who designed the original Parliament Building in Ottawa, the Post Office in Galt was a magnificent showpiece of High Victorian architecture and an ingenious display of masonry craftsmanship. The use of contrasting stones—grey and red granite fieldstones with light-grey limestone trim—and the tantalizing array of masonry techniques—smooth, rough-faced, and sculpted—combined into a bold yet delightful composition that is further animated by large brackets, a front gable, and clock tower. The building summarizes the amazing potential of stone when in the hands of master masons.

Even though more than a century of development has occurred since its remarkable "era of stone," the city still retains a critical mass of this heritage, symbolized in the towered City Hall, steepled churches, business district, and vast industrial complexes. Yet, in addition to these prominent monuments, it is surprising how many modest stone buildings one discovers around the corner, time after time, which build up a genuine picture of this once Scottish stone town, the pride of its early settlers. The Grand River, still the featured centrepiece of the city, contributes significantly to this sense of continuity with the past.

The former Galt Post Office excelled in architectural ornamentation with its wide range of textures and designs carved in the limestone trim.

Paris

Approximately twenty-three kilometres downstream from Galt at the confluence of the Grand and Nith Rivers, a new settlement took root in 1829. First called the Forks of the Grand River, the place was well-known for the extraordinary beauty of its forested heights, steep slopes, and converging rivers. The original settler, William Holme, had arrived in 1821 with the romantic vision of taming the wilderness into a country estate in the manner of the English landed gentry. In 1823, Hiram Capron arrived at Holme's log cabin with ironware for sale from his nearby foundry. Capron reminisced later about this first visit: "I gazed spellbound upon the beautiful valley, then in its natural beauty and rugged grandeur, before the axe had robbed it of its stately oaks and wide-spreading elms. And before mounting my horse, I made up my mind to own this lovely vale." By 1829, the hardships of frontier life had proven too much for Holme, and he willingly sold 1,000 acres to the persistent Capron for the amount equivalent to $10,000. Born in Vermont, Hiram Capron was the quintessential pioneer adventurer—resourceful, indefatigable and fearless. He had worked his way across upper New York state, learning different trades as he went. In Manchester, New York, he had learned the foundry business. In 1822, with the support of four partners, he purchased and managed the Normandale Furnace on the north shore of Lake Erie. So successful was the iron foundry in producing household ironware and cooking stoves that Capron became wealthy enough to purchase his "lovely vale" at the Forks of the Grand and establish a new community.

Left: Unlike any other cobblestone house in the Paris area, Kilton Cottage was designed in the Gothic Revival style, complete with its signature pointed-arched windows and decorative bargeboard. It was built in 1857 for David Patton and his bride.

St. James Anglican Church of 1839 is Paris's oldest cobblestone building and marks the beginning of this Paris specialty that lasted until the early 1860s. The fieldstone chancel was added in 1863, and the new entrance in 1990.

The site promised not only abundant water power and a land route to Lake Ontario (Governor's Road to Dundas), but also a marketable natural resource—gypsum deposits—that could be mined and pulverized to make either plaster of Paris or fertilizer. In 1830, Capron hired a surveyor to lay out the first town lots, which he offered free to settlers. He also proposed to change the long name of Forks of the Grand River to Paris, after its plaster supply. It was said villagers shrank "from Paris, a name associated with mobs, guillotines, and ambitious ladies," but agreed to it one year later. A Vermonter and descendent of a long line of adventurous pioneers, Capron then directed his enterprising spirit towards developing his plaster exports (1,000 tons in 1850) and attracting new settlers, many from western New York state, by building a dam and race, plaster and grist mills, and improving Governor's Road. King Capron, as he was called, was also known for his unfailing generosity to people in need. He was never known to have foreclosed on a mortgage.

Among the American immigrants attracted to Paris was the stonemason Levi Boughton who arrived in 1838 from Normandale, New York, after spending three years in Brantford. It was Boughton who is credited with establishing a remarkable and rare stone heritage in Paris—cobblestone architecture. Boughton is thought to have built (with assistance) most of Paris's cobblestone buildings. Paris, although today a town of predominantly brick buildings, does have a remarkable and rare stone heritage of its own—cobblestone architecture. Surprisingly durable, cobblestones form a veneer on a rubblestone wall that was usually limited to public (front and side) façades—in the hands of a skilled mason they create a beautiful, rhythmically textured, natural surface that rises to the level of folk art. Only two places in Ontario have a concentration of cobblestone buildings—Paris and Belleville—both of which had close ties with the Rochester, New York area where the method first appeared in the northern United States. Used historically in England, cobblestone architecture was perfected across western New York state from the 1830s to the 1860s by masons who were looking for work after the Erie Canal was completed in 1825. One proud homeowner in

St. James Anglican Church.

New York state wrote in 1835, "The stone I do not consider any expense as it frees the land of them. There is no painting to be done to it, as is required of brick or wood, it makes the strongest of walls, and I think the neatest and cheapest building that can be made." That the counties around Rochester still have over 700 cobblestone buildings establishes it as the North American centre for this construction method, and attests to its wide appeal and durability.

Cobbles are stones rounded by glacial or water action, often measuring about four to eight centimetres thick and eighteen to twenty-two centimetres long. They say a cobble can be held in the palm of a hand, a pebble between two fingers, and a boulder with two hands. Cobblestones, mostly formed of sedimentary stone, occurred regularly in farmers' fields and along watercourses. Construction was precise, painstaking work that could take up to five years to complete. First, the smoothed cobblestones were collected, sorted by colour, and sized by putting them through an iron ring or a board with the correct-sized

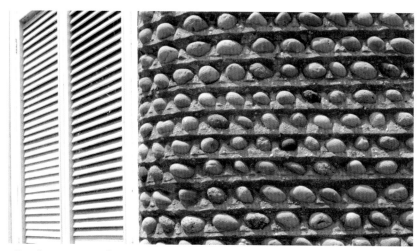

Sowden Home and Dispensary, built in the 1840s, illustrates mason Levi Boughton's skill in carrying the rows of cobblestones smoothly around the curved corner, a feature rarely found in this type of masonry.

hole; then, a highly skilled mason laid them at right angles to the building in horizontal rows. They were embedded into a thick mortar, separated by a continuous, raised, horizontal V-shaped line. Longer cobbles might be bonded directly into the rubblestone wall behind. In and around Paris, twelve houses and two churches acquired cobblestone veneer; one house has been demolished.

This technique appeared early in Paris's history with the building of St. James Anglican Church in 1839. Money raised for the Paris building came from Scottish and English supporters with the condition that it be an Anglican church and built of stone. Without stone quarries nearby, Paris was fortunate that master mason Levi Boughton had arrived the year before, bringing with him the technical skills of building in cobblestone that he had learned in the Rochester area. St. James is Paris's first cobblestone building and represents an amazing accomplishment by Boughton, given the two-year timeline and the size of the project. The work must have relied on extensive assistance from others. The stones, said to be collected from the hillside across the Grand River, are somewhat

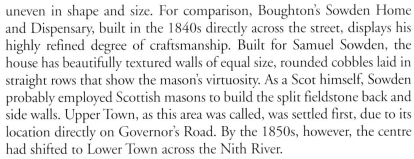

Hamilton Place has an 1844 date-stone over the front door and second-storey eyebrow windows behind the veranda. It is estimated that it took 32,000 cobblestones and five years to build Hamilton Place.

uneven in shape and size. For comparison, Boughton's Sowden Home and Dispensary, built in the 1840s directly across the street, displays his highly refined degree of craftsmanship. Built for Samuel Sowden, the house has beautifully textured walls of equal size, rounded cobbles laid in straight rows that show the mason's virtuosity. As a Scot himself, Sowden probably employed Scottish masons to build the split fieldstone back and side walls. Upper Town, as this area was called, was settled first, due to its location directly on Governor's Road. By the 1850s, however, the centre had shifted to Lower Town across the Nith River.

It was north of Lower Town, albeit on a ridge as high as Upper Town, where Norman Hamilton, the driving American business man (described in 1883 as a "pushing, independent, succeed-at-any-price Yankee," but also "an able and amiable man"), built his mansion Hamilton Place (originally known as Hillside) in 1844. Hamilton, having arrived in Paris in 1831 (the first year after lots became

available), soon came to dominate the economic life of the town with his shrewd purchases of mills and the development of a distillery (selling whiskey at fifteen cents a gallon on the Toronto market). This he combined with a pork-packing factory, the happy pigs being fed on the mash left over from the whiskey-making process. Hamilton, who came from Mendon, New York, where the use of both cobblestone and the Greek Revival style was in fashion, chose Boughton to build his stately home in cobblestone (on all four façades) and architect Andrew Minny to design a full-fashioned Doric "temple." Complete with a series of wooden veranda piers and a belvedere to light the upstairs rooms, Hamilton Place is Paris's prized monument of cobblestone architecture, an ideal union of setting, craftsmanship, and architectural design.

Down the hill, the town acquired another cobblestone Greek temple in the 1840s, the Mitchell House, also built for a fellow New Yorker by Levi Boughton. Here the design, more modest in scale yet still sophisticated, includes a carved stone entrance porch, stone corner piers, and eyebrow windows in the cornice to light the upstairs bedrooms, again assisted by a belvedere. The water-rounded cobbles are remarkably similar in size and shape (said to have been gathered personally by the original owner from the nearby Nith River). Boughton did a masterful job of placing them evenly in rows; on the front façade the oval stones are all slanted to the left, creating an elegant textured pattern. This building is considered Boughton's finest example of cobblestone work.

Back in Upper Town, Levi Boughton built another cobblestone house, the Bosworth House, from 1842–1845, for Reverend Newton Alfred Bosworth which was later sold to the Baptist Church to use as its manse. In 1870, when the Reverend Thomas Henderson was residing there, Melville Bell and his family, including son Alexander Graham Bell, arrived from Scotland and lived there a few months before

Upper left: The Mitchell House, built in the 1840s, is considered the finest example of Levi Boughton's cobblestone work.
Left: The 1845 Bosworth House hosted Alexander Graham Bell in 1870.

eventually settling in Brantford. Sitting on a hillside overlooking the town, Bosworth's story and a half cottage is also one of a kind: it is generously large and has an unusual truncated gable roof as well as a decorative Victorian porch. If it is true that the master mason actually worked on all the buildings credited to his name, then it is not surprising that his own home, the Levi Boughton House, was not built until 1851–1852. For his own house, Boughton chose the one-storey, five-bay Ontario Cottage, a type popular with masons and carpenters.

In 1850, with a population of 1,000, Paris officially became a village, and in 1856 a town. By then, Hiram Capron had become a wealthy man (his holdings were estimated at $250,000.), as well as a generous philanthropist, donating funds or land to churches, the library, and other needy causes. As did other communities along the Grand River, Paris got an economic boost from the arrival of the railway—the Great Western Railway in 1854 (Hamilton to Windsor) and the Fort Erie–Goderich line in 1856. As a junction of two lines, Paris became a shipping centre for goods either manufactured in town or routed through town. The railways also attracted the establishment of major new industries in the

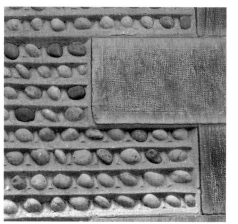

Levi Boughton House, built in 1851–1852 by the stonemason for his family, is a charming Ontario Cottage that housed his family for over 30 years. The unevenness of execution suggests that Levi's son, a mason in training, did some of the work due to his father's heavy workload.

1860s such as the Penman Manufacturing Company, Paris's successful textile mills.

By this time alternative masonry construction was making its appearance in town as cobblestone work began to decline: founder Hiram Capron built a handsome limestone mansion in the 1850s resembling the fine townhouses of Hamilton (in fact, the stone is said to have come from Ancaster, possibly transported on the new rail line), but unfortunately in the 1880s it was almost entirely absorbed into John Penman's grandiose High Victorian castle, Penmarvian. Squared stone was likewise used for the inn and house the brothers James and Charles Miller built at 22–24 Dumfries Street in the early 1850s in Upper Town. Solid, unadorned, and well-proportioned, this type of fieldstone construction was uncommon in Paris. A rare experimentation into

Top: The Dumfries St. row is one of Paris's finest fieldstone examples.
Left: Gouinlock House is a rare example of masonry experimentation.

masonry construction can be found in the charming Ontario Cottage known as the Gouinlock House, built in the early 1850s for merchant W. Gouinlock. It is described as having a rubblestone core with a layer of coarse (pre-modern) concrete poured as a facing on both inside and outside surfaces while the walls were being built. The exterior was then parged in a handsome ashlar design that is remarkably convincing. Another noteworthy stone structure in Paris is the Sacred Heart Roman Catholic Church, built in 1857; the corner tower was added in 1880. With its coursed, multi-coloured fieldstone and animated Gothic Revival design, the church was described in 1883 as "the architectural glory of this part of town."

Although cobblestone houses were not built in town after the early 1850s—the Anglican rectory was an exception—they continued to be erected in the rural area just north of Paris. The earliest cobblestone structure was a small Wesleyan Methodist chapel known as the Paris Plains Church,

Top: The Paris Plains Church was completed in 1845. Its fine gothic windows and textured cobblestone walls give it an enduring beauty.
Right: Sacred Heart Roman Catholic Church is a splendid fieldstone work.

Top: George Brown Farmhouse, built during the late 1850s, is a classic five-bay home, that resembles a cobblestone prototype found in western New York state. Bottom: The Deans Farmhouse, built in 1862 for Mary and Matthew Deans, is a cobblestone house that has remained in the same family for five generations.

completed in 1845 about five kilometres out of town. It is a remarkable work of folk art, built by volunteers using stones from the surrounding fields. The tall, multi-paned Gothic windows and the richly textured cobblestone walls delightfully enliven this very simple, intimate structure. Credited with supervising the work, mason Levi Boughton had succeeded in training his assistants well, for the structure has proven durable. When under threat of demolition in 1948, it was saved and restored by a group of volunteers (they replaced 414 panes of glass). Today, the church appears much as it did originally, a small gem on the rural landscape of South Dumfries Township. In the area nearby, a series of farmhouses were constructed in cobblestone, each one different, yet all illustrating a mastery of the material. The George Brown House, built in the late 1850s, is a classic, one-and-a-half-storey farmhouse that was given new significance through the beauty of its evenly textured walls. By comparison, Kilton Cottage demonstrates how delightfully the picturesque quality of the Gothic Revival combines with the lively nature of the cobblestone surface. Built for David Patton in 1857, the house features pointed-arched windows, a bay window, finials, and decorative bargeboards that add to the play of light and shadow on the textured walls. The Deans Farmhouse, completed ca. 1862 for Matthew and Mary Deans, represents the three-bay farmhouse that became the most popular design in Ontario (in this case, the front gable is a later addition). That it is now owned by Matthew's great-great-grandson and is still operating as a farm shows a remarkable continuity. Matthew Deans came from Paisley, Scotland, yet he chose to build the family homestead in cobblestone, proving that it was not only the preference of Yankee settlers. John Maus, a farmer whose family had settled the Paris Plains (sometimes called Maus Plains) embarked on building an entirely different homestead. He chose multi-coloured, split-granite masonry and stately dimensions for his home, the John Maus House, built ca.1860. Complete with an attached kitchen wing and coachhouse of matching stonework, this homestead looks more like an estate complex than a rural farmhouse. The quality throughout suggests the work of a talented architect and skilled craftsmen. The lintels with carved keystone and sills are of limestone from Guelph; the windows are generously wide; the granite fieldstone is squared and coursed; and the interior work in wood and plaster is executed with considerable finesse.

Left: Kilton Cottage Bottom: John Maus House was built ca. 1860 using granite and Guelph limestone in its construction. The house is an exceptionally refined and stylish work of architecture that has been beautifully restored by the present owner.

Although Paris can claim several fine limestone and fieldstone buildings, clearly its specialty was cobblestone architecture. Just as the granite masonry of Galt is tied to its Scottish culture, Paris owes its cobblestone work to the influx of American settlers from western New York state and to one master mason in particular, Levi Boughton. As an excessively labour-intensive, time-consuming work, cobblestone masonry ceased by the mid-1860s, replaced by the cheaper and more fashionable brick. By then, Lower Town had far surpassed Upper Town with its one hundred businesses, and manufacturing had become more diversified, including the growing textile industry. The cobblestone era already belonged to the distant past, but these hardy, durable structures did not succumb. Now, a century and a half later, they are recognized for their uniqueness and artistry: these thirteen buildings bear witness to the resourcefulness and character of Paris's early settlers.

Ancaster-Dundas-Flamborough

The rock-faced hills of Ancaster and Flamborough (known locally as the "mountain") and the beautiful Dundas Valley that lies between them comprise an area that has a rich architectural heritage in stone. This legacy, scattered throughout the valley and farmlands, in the small hamlets, villages, and towns, is not intensely concentrated in any one place, but accumulatively constitutes a valued resource. The defining geographical feature of southern Ontario, the stone mass of the Niagara Escarpment, curves around the western end of Lake Ontario, interrupted at the Dundas Valley. Building in stone first became a common practice when skilled stonemasons arrived in the late 1840s. Stone was quarried from both above and below the escarpment—stonemasons building in "mountain" communities (Ancaster, Waterdown, and West Flamborough) generally used limestone quarried locally from bedrock, while in places below the escarpment (Dundas), they mostly used sandstone where it was quarried. The difficulty of carting heavy blocks of stone any distance, especially up and down the mountain, accounts primarily for this general distribution—but sandstone trim and even sandstone façades can also be found above the escarpment. As elsewhere, the use of rubblestone for the less visible side(s) and back was the norm. It is curious that none of these settlements became a full-fledged stone town in the way Guelph, Fergus, Galt, or St. Marys did, even though local quarries were numerous. Perhaps this is partly due to the continuous availability of affordable brick, which by the late 1870s had replaced

The former Ancaster Township Hall, built in 1871, has Italianate features adopted to the traditional town hall design. When the new Township Hall was built in 1966, a citizens' group took the lead in saving and restoring the building for community use

The Union Hotel in Ancaster, built in 1832 for George Rousseau, and the adjacent stone stables sit with gable-ends to the street and could almost be expecting a stagecoach to arrive, were it not for their twentieth-century conversion to store and apartment uses.

stone in popularity. Also, wood was commonly used in smaller communities. Yet, during its heyday, the area's quarried stone formed a sizable and varied heritage that can only be represented by a few samples from each area. These are not enough to give a portrait of their respective communities, just a brief introduction. In 2000, Ancaster, Dundas, and Flamborough were amalgamated into the City of Hamilton.

Places where swift-flowing streams cascaded over the escarpment became the sites of three major pioneer settlements: Ancaster on Ancaster Mill Creek and Waterdown on Grindstone Creek—both on the escarpment—and Dundas on Spencer Creek below the falls.

First to settle above the escarpment at the future site of Ancaster, even before it was surveyed, was millwright James Wilson in 1784. With fur trader Richard Beasley, he built the first grist mill in the area

Fairview in Ancaster was built in 1859 by the English-born country squire Thomas Bush for his daughter on the occasion of her marriage to Dr. Henry Orton on lands belonging to his own estate next door at Springfield (now Brockton, known also as the Young Estate).

in 1791. By 1794, Wilson had sold his share to the enterprising, 37-year-old Jean-Baptiste Rousseau, another fur trader, friend of Joseph Brant, interpreter for Native peoples, and a fifth-generation Quebecer. J. B. Rousseau, known as St. Jean, opened a store, purchased more mills, and established a hotel, but died of pleurisy in the War of 1812 at age 55. His son, George, carried on the family tradition by building the Union Hotel in 1832 and the next-door Stone Stables in the heart of the village. The hotel, enlarged at the back in 1854, is distinguished by its squared limestone façade, wooden balcony across the front, and fanciful bargeboard trim. The family's imprint on the village continued in 1848 when St. Jean's grandson, George Brock Rousseau, built the handsome limestone house across the street (now the Rousseau House restaurant).

Some of the finest stone villas ever built at the Head-of-the-Lake were located in Ancaster Township in the verdant rolling landscape of the Dundas Valley, an area that has been largely preserved in its natural state. Among a number of the fine limestone houses in the valley is

The Old Ancaster Mill, built in 1863 as the fourth mill on the site, has proven itself not only durable, but also adaptable when a new restaurant was added across the stream to its historic complex of miller's home and mill.

Fairview, a private estate comprising a Gothic Revival house of 1859, a carriage house, and beautifully landscaped grounds. Another is the splendid Woodend (not shown), the present headquarters of the Hamilton Conservation Authority, which was originally built for John Heslop in 1862. Both Fairview and Woodend share the distinction of having triple gables across the front façade with bargeboard and triangular windows on the second floor, an unusual feature also occasionally found in Hamilton villas of the era.

The years around Confederation saw a variety of beautiful stone buildings erected in Ancaster village, one of the most prominent being the Old Ancaster Mill, a grist mill located just downstream from Wilson's founding mill. Standing three-and-a-half-storeys high, this massive limestone structure was built in 1863 by Alonzo and Harris Egleston, the fourth mill to be constructed on the same site. Typical of mill construction, the walls were built of uncoursed, irregular-sized limestone, which was strengthened at the corners by large quoins. A flurry of church building also occurred at this time: St. Andrew's Presbyterian Church (1874); the New Zion Church (1869, now the chapel for Ryerson Church); and directly across the street, St. John's Anglican Church, built of locally quarried limestone in 1869 after fire had destroyed its 1826 frame structure. The new structure was designed by Toronto architects Gundry and Langley in the Gothic Revival style, highly reminiscent of the traditional English parish church, with its tall bell tower, steep gable roof, and low side walls. Nearby and just two years later, architect Albert Hills of Hamilton designed the Ancaster Township Hall. Contractor William Thuresson erected the building in coursed limestone for $2,700. The youngest of the area township halls, it is distinguished from the earlier ones by a spacious front lawn and Italianate features charmingly combined—a two-staged belfry, an extra tall doorway with fanlight, and a prominent Tuscan-columned portico.

Across the valley, a natural place for a mill settlement to take hold was along Spencer Creek as it tumbled its way down off the escarpment and out to the marsh and bay beyond. Here, Dundas founder Richard Hatt erected a grist mill, the New Dundas Mills (1804–1968), the first to serve the farmers of the hinterland from as far away as Waterloo County. This site had other advantages too: given its location at the westernmost end of Lake Ontario, Lieutenant-Governor Simcoe in 1793 saw it as the eastern terminus for the route to his new capital (London) in the wilderness at the Thames River (when Simcoe left in 1797, York was chosen as the capital). Peter Desjardins in 1826 proposed to link Dundas to Lake Ontario via a canal through the marsh of Cootes Paradise (it was finally opened in 1837 but soon lost business to the new railways in the 1850s). Yet these three assets—the water power of Spencer Creek, the marsh's access to Lake Ontario, and the escarpment's stone for quarrying—brought such prosperity to Dundas that by 1847 it was officially incorporated as a town. The local council approved designs by Francis Hawkins for the new Dundas Town Hall, and contractor James Scott built it in 1849 of locally

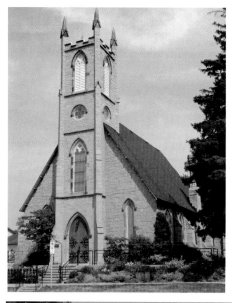

Left: St. John's Anglican Church in Ancaster was built in 1869 to the designs of architects Gundry and Langley. The church still retains its original cemetery. Situated on a height of land at the western end of town, St. John's tower is a prominent focal point of the village.
Below: Ancaster Township Hall.

Above: The former Dundas Town Hall, designed by Francis Hawkins, was built in 1849 by James Scott. Typically, the town hall was multipurpose: the upstairs, high-ceilinged room served as council chamber, ball room, and auditorium; the main floor as offices; and the basement as butcher stalls, tavern, and jail. Right and upper right: Wood-Dale in Dundas was built in ashlar sandstone in 1846. Characterized by a façade of full-length windows and a vine-covered veranda (since removed), the Regency cottage was a favourite of British colonials.

quarried sandstone. (Interestingly, Scott's bid to build in stone at £1,870 was slightly less than in brick at £1,986.) This early public building, distinguished by its cupola, represents one of the finest achievements of masonry work in the town, with walls elegantly articulated with two-storey Doric pilasters and arched window surrounds.

Although the town's early stone mills and churches have been lost and the builders of the shopping district preferred brick, Dundas still possesses a wonderfully varied collection of about three dozen stone houses, large and small, dating mostly from its formative years around the 1840s and 1850s. From this we can glean a sense of pre-Confederation Dundas—who the builders were and what their tastes were. The original owner of Wood-Dale was a Scottish merchant Thomas McKenzie, traveller, adventurer, and commander in the Rebellion of 1837. When Lieutenant-Colonel McKenzie settled down in Dundas, he built a quintessential Regency cottage in 1846 in local sandstone. A ballroom was added in 1876. The stonework of Wood-Dale is remarkable for its unusually wide ashlar blocks

and its classical doorframe with Doric pilasters. A few years later and across town, it was the lawyer, aspiring politician, and future judge on the Upper Court of Ontario, Thomas Robertson, who built a stately two-storey stone residence, Foxbar, set back from Governor's Road on a height of land. Also of Scottish parentage and privileged background, Robertson came to Hamilton to join a law firm in 1852, when he presumably began building his Dundas residence. With its generous proportions, wide central doorway, and double-arched window above, Foxbar is a splendid, gracious home. The masonry is intricately laid: the squared, coursed sandstone blocks are filled in with narrow vertical rows of matching small stones (nogging). A third Scot, but in this case a self-made businessman and the

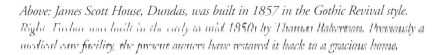

Above: James Scott House, Dundas, was built in 1857 in the Gothic Revival style. Right: Foxbar was built in the early to mid 1850s by Thomas Robertson. Previously a medical care facility, the present owners have restored it back to a gracious home.

250–252 King Street West, Dundas, is dated 1857 in its keystone. Recently restored, the house reveals the beauty of a cut sandstone façade, attributed to English stonecutter William Millward, who had arrived in Dundas as early as 1835.

contractor for the Dundas Town Hall, built his own home, the James Scott House, in 1857 in another popular style of the time, the Gothic Revival. The front sandstone façade displays a rich pattern of small and larger stones laid in broken courses, with a subtle use of quoins at the corners and around the windows and doorway (a device more commonly found in Galt). However, it was not only the well-to-do who built the stone houses in Dundas: many houses were one-storey workmen's cottages of fine proportions, and a few were semi-detached houses, built for investment purposes, such as the one at 250–252 King Street West dated 1857 (in the keystone), for tax collector Patrick Quinn. Attributed to the English stonecutter William Millward, the stones were laid in a subtle pattern and so tightly fitted together that the surface is smooth and clean, with only the transoms adding a decorative note.

While Flamborough's political boundaries have changed in both name and size over the years, the term is used here to refer to East and West Flamborough Townships. It encompasses farmland, numerous small hamlets, and villages that include a variety of fine stone farmhouses, churches, houses, schoolhouses, and three township halls. Historic Waterdown Village still retains a rich heritage of at least nineteen stone buildings built before 1872, primarily of local limestone, some with sandstone features. The following sampling includes three buildings from Waterdown, two houses from West Flamboro' Village area, and one farmhouse in East Flamborough Township.

Waterdown began to grow with the arrival in 1823 of the enterprising Ebenezer Culver Griffin, of American parentage and firm Methodists beliefs. He bought 158 acres on Grindstone Creek from Alexander Brown, known to the area's Native peoples since 1805 as the "white man of the mountain." By 1831, Griffin was offering town lots. Two more sawmills, a carding mill, and another grist mill developed along the raceways, and a core settlement began taking shape at the main crossroads of Mill and Dundas Streets. While none of Ebenezer's own buildings has survived, the homestead of his eldest son (James Kent Griffin) has. Set on a lovely height, the main part of the Griffin House was constructed in irregularly sized limestone in the 1860s, a home large enough for raising his eleven children.

He faced the original frame structure of 1844 with stone and built additions as needed. As did his industrious father before him, Griffin dedicated himself to the village's forward progress, including becoming a contractor for building houses and roads (Snake Road, 1853–1854, became Waterdown's first toll road to Hamilton). In addition to his other roles, J. K. was appointed Clerk of the new Township of East Flamborough when it was established in 1850. Subsequently, the East Flamborough Township Hall, now the Waterdown Library, was erected in 1857 in the heart of the village. Constructed to the plans and specifications of stonemason Walter Grieve, the handsome two-storey hall is typically placed gable-end to the street. Its presence is further enhanced by the erection of a smaller version directly next door in 1865—the Weslyan Methodist Church, now the Waterdown Alliance Church. So popular was Methodism at the western end of Lake Ontario that the area became known as "Methodist Mountain." These two buildings together form a unique focal point for Waterdown's heritage in stone.

Left: The former East Flamborough Township Hall in Waterdown was constructed in 1857 of coursed limestone with sandstone trim. The graceful, arched, second-storey window and octagonal wooden belfry earn it a special place among the rural southern Ontario municipal halls.

Above: Griffin House in Waterdown is distinguished architecturally by its unusual slanted (jerkin) gable roof with paired chimneys front and back. The original 1844 frame section was faced in stone to match the main 1860s stone house. The home with its later extensions sits comfortably on its spacious lot of tall trees.

Near the little village of West Flamboro' on the old Dundas–Waterloo Road (now Highway 8) stand two stone houses erected in the mid-nineteenth century that illustrate well the exceptional quality of design and mastery of stonework found in country houses—the one-and-a-half-storey Stonegates and the two-storey Stormont, each set well back from the road. Although of different styles, they both were built by the 1850s of local limestone with sandstone quoins and voussoirs that had to be hauled up the "mountain." Even more surprising to find on a back concession road of East Flamborough Township is the remarkable, patterned Blagdon Farmhouse built in 1862 by stonemason Thomas Le Mesurier, who lived on a farm nearby and built two other farmhouses in

The former Weslyan Methodist Church in Waterdown was built in limestone in 1865. The design specialized in using round-headed arches, which gave the builder the opportunity to use elegant sandstone voussoirs throughout the building (that are actually aligned to the fan-like fenestration).

the neighbourhood. The combination of dark limestone with light sandstone achieved an unusual banding effect that is especially noticeable on the Blagdon House's two-storey façade. This Georgian house type dates back to the United Empire Loyalist homes of the early 1800s, curiously, the same model that was used in the Mennonite houses in the 1860s in Wilmot Township.

This introduction to the Ancaster-Dundas-Flamborough area is intended to give a brief glimpse into the richness of the stone heritage that resides there. Of endless interest are the variations in building types, architectural styles, and local building stone. While it was Hamilton's success to grow exponentially from port settlement (1832) to railway hub (1854), and, ultimately, into a major industrial city of the late nineteenth and twentieth centuries, its expansion may have helped save the small-town scale and nineteenth-century cores of these outlying communities. Except for the loss of industrial buildings experienced everywhere, the stone heritage of this area has survived remarkably intact and is well worth further exploration.

Upper left: Stonegates in West Flamboro' Village was built in limestone and sandstone.

Top: Stormont in West Flamboro' Village was built nearby by William Miller

Bottom: Blagdon House in East Flamborough was built in a banded stone pattern.

Hamilton

Of all the communities included in this book, Hamilton ranks as the largest in size and perhaps the most unexpected choice. Because of its explosive population growth from 25,000 in the mid-1800s to 250,000 by the mid-1900s, the picturesque stone town of the 1850s soon was over-trumped by the robust, High Victorian city of the 1890s, which, in turn, was swallowed up by the expanded, modernized city of the twentieth century. With redevelopment occurring often in the historic part of town, Hamilton would appear at first glance to have lost its 1850s stone heritage; closer inspection reveals a remarkable resource, which, although reduced and scattered, includes some of the most exceptional stone buildings ever built in southwestern Ontario.

While a few settlers had arrived in the area in the 1780s, including fur-trader Richard Beasley and Loyalist Robert Land, Hamilton began as a community in 1816 when the province approved a proposed townsite on the farm bought by George Hamilton (son of Queenston's founder Robert Hamilton) the year before. In part because of the Hamilton family political and social connections, the Upper Canada government chose this settlement to be the county seat for the new District of Gore, winning out over heavy opposition from the older communities of Dundas and Ancaster. Hamilton's first role was as a judicial and administrative centre, symbolized by the construction of the new stone Gore District Courthouse completed in 1832.

The location of the new settlement offered considerable natural advantages: it was situated on a harbour at the western end of Lake

The virtuoso display of masonry skills in the Hamilton Custom House was due to master mason George Worthington. The project was approved when Hamilton's Sir Allan Napier MacNab was prime minister, and built in 1858–1860 using Frederick Rubidge's plans.

Whitehern, a Classical Revival mansion, built ca. 1850, became the family home for three generations of the McQuesten family. In 1958, Whitehern was bequeathed to Hamilton and is now open as an historic house museum.

Ontario, which only needed a cut through the sand spit known as Burlington Beach to make it accessible to lake traffic. By 1832, the Burlington Canal connected the lake to the deepwater port of Hamilton and inaugurated a shipping industry that still prospers today. The site also incorporated the high stony bluff of the Niagara Escarpment that in some places reaches a height of one hundred metres, a future source of stone for building roads and structures. Geographically, Hamilton was close enough to the American border to attract adventurous entrepreneurs; it was also strategically positioned to supply western expansion in the farming hinterland. Although the new settlement had water access, it lacked water power produced by fast-moving rivers and waterfalls, in contrast to the traditional pioneer settlements that started with the building of grist and saw mills along the rivers.

Settlers began arriving in numbers in the 1830s, among them enterprising young men sent out from Scotland or Scottish firms in Montreal to establish westernmost offices for their trading companies back home, as Colin Ferrie had done for his father, the Honourable Adam Ferrie. Some were attracted to the judicial functions of the settlement, among whom was lawyer Allan Napier MacNab, who like many others combined his professional work with land development investments. American settlers also came, looking for new opportunities on the frontier, including John Fisher, who, with the support of his uncle, Dr. Calvin McQuesten, set up a foundry to manufacture cast-iron agricultural implements and stoves. Such an industry, which eventually provided the basis for steel manufacturing, was well-suited to Hamilton because its production relied on transporting materials to and from the harbour, but did not require a source of water power which Hamilton lacked. In 1833, Hamilton was incorporated as a town, marking its beginning as a self-regulating municipality.

The seeds that were sown in the 1830s came to fruition in the 1850s. The incorporation of Hamilton as a city in 1846 kicked off a decade of unprecedented growth and prosperity, with its population jumping from 9,889 in 1848 to 25,000 in 1857. The arrival of the Great Western Railway in 1854 fuelled a new railway boom. Many of the young merchants of the 1830s had achieved considerable wealth by the late 1840s, as had their industrialist counterparts. Hamilton had come of age and was poised to become a community of significance. Just at this time, numerous skilled British masons, hearing of Hamilton's building boom and productive local quarries, came to the area looking for work. Stone became the principal building material during the next ten years that saw every type of building constructed—from the most modest cottage to the most sophisticated public edifice. Hamilton quarries produced a fine Whirlpool sandstone (sometimes called freestone because it could be cut in any direction) popular for façades; limestone was also used. As elsewhere, rubblestone was traditionally used for the side and rear walls.

The harbinger of Hamilton's "stone age" boom was the building of private residences by the well-to-do: Hamilton's first mayor, Colin Ferrie, had built Westlawn as early as 1836 (demolished 1957). By the late 1840s, a cluster of dignified residences and splendid villa estates began to appear south of the business district, some commandeering the lower slopes of the escarpment. Interestingly, in Hamilton, whether one was Scottish, English, or American did not seem to determine one's choice of architectural styles or building material—all preferred building in stone at this momentous time, some favouring styles of classical inspiration, some Gothic. Whitehern, situated in the heart of the modern city, was built ca. 1850. Dr. Calvin McQuesten (who with John Fisher helped found the iron industry in Hamilton) and his family had moved in by 1852. Their descendants continued living at Whitehern until 1958, when it was bequeathed by the family to the city. Symmetrical and self-contained, the residence, constructed of Whirlpool sandstone, sits on a raised terrace, presenting a picture of dignity and permanence with its elaborate front porch offering a gracious welcome to the outside world. When Scottish merchant Archibald Kerr chose to build his home ca.1850, he hired the leading architect of the time, William Thomas, to build a Gothic Revival villa in stone, Inglewood, on a twelve-acre country estate high up on the slopes of the escarpment. Symmetrical yet picturesque, Gothic fancy

Whitehern entrance.

Rosemount Cottage, a Gothic Revival villa designed by William Thomas and built ca. 1850, was one of at least seven rival villa estates, all built in stone along the upper slopes of the Niagara Escarpment. Hamilton was once renowned for its legacy of elegant country estates, four of which survive.

mixed with stone solidity, Kerr's thirty-room castle in all its splendour reigned over the city below. While the exterior's pointed-arched windows and doorway were a stately version of the Gothic style, the main interior rooms enjoyed a stunning, virtuoso display of craftsmanship in the wood mouldings, fireplaces, staircase, and the ceiling's curvilinear plasterwork. Inglewood was William Thomas's Gothic villa masterpiece.

Not only did the founding fathers spearhead the city's economic development, they also actively promoted its cultural and religious life. The province had just taken on the responsibility of providing a regulated system of public education with the passage of the *Common*

Central Public School, built in 1853 and designed by architects Cumberland and Ridout, incorporates Egerton Ryerson's reforms to provide equal education to all. The 1890 expansion included building a High Victorian tower. Central School still continues to function as a public school.

School Acts in 1846 and 1850. In 1853, Hamilton met the challenge boldly by building the first, large, graded Central Public School in British North America. Located in the heart of the downtown, the new school, constructed of local sandstone, was designed to give equal education to a thousand students, rich and poor, girls as well as boys. The Toronto architectural firm Cumberland and Ridout` designed the landmark building as a two-storey, symmetrical, central-towered structure in the Classical Revival style, establishing a prototype that became widespread. At the mid-century mark, churches also began replacing their earlier frame buildings of the 1830s with larger stone edifices. The Presbyterian church members in 1854 embarked on a remarkably ambitious new scheme for St. Andrew's, later St. Paul's Presbyterian Church, a high-styled Gothic Revival church designed by Toronto's leading architect, William Thomas. It featured a soaring, fifty-five-metre-high spire of stone, to be completed within three years by master mason George Worthington. Considered Thomas's finest ecclesiastical work and the best example of its type in Ontario, the church, constructed primarily in local sandstone, has strong perpendicular lines, massive buttresses, stone carvings, and traceried windows that captured the essence of the Decorated Gothic Revival

St. Paul's Presbyterian Church, built in 1854–1857 to the plans of William Thomas, is recognized as a masterpiece of the Decorated Gothic Revival style. The sandstone church has a fifty-five-metre-high stone spire, said to be the only stone spire ever built in the province.

style. (Stone for the spire was imported from Ohio.) The church's interior with its carved dark woodwork and stained-glass windows still retains the quiet, mysterious ambiance of its original design.

As the quarries increased the supply of building material and stonemasons grew in numbers during the early 1850s, building in stone became accessible and affordable for all: the labourer could build a cottage, or the merchant a fashionable terrace house. The James Street Terrace, built in 1854–1860, represents the many stone rows that once lined Hamilton streets. So strong was the imprint of the rowhouse on British immigrants that isolated terraces would appear in the midst of empty fields in expectation that someday the city would expand to meet them. Built with ashlar sandstone façades, this ten-unit terrace provided single-family housing for business people and professionals. The paragon of the mid-nineteenth-century stone terrace is Hamilton's Sandyford Place, built in 1858–1862 by Scottish stonemason Donald Nicholson. The three-storey, four-house terrace of palazzo design (with the end units projecting forward) is a masterpiece of masonry work:

local ashlar sandstone provided the background for the finely sculpted lintels, scroll brackets, and corner quoins that defined the Classical—in this case Renaissance—Revival style. Proportions are on the grand scale, creating a dignified, fashionable terrace that would fit on the best streets of Edinburgh or Glasgow.

With its port serving the Great Lakes, and its railway connecting to New York state and Michigan (the Great Western Railway, 1854), Hamilton was perfectly positioned to develop an overseas transshipment business and a wholesale market for western expansion. The large-scale operations of these wholesale firms led the owners to build massive "mercantile palaces" to serve as warehouses: the most significant one of all, the Commercial Block, built in 1856 for the wholesale dry goods firm of Young, Law & Co., is the only one to survive. Designed by Frederick Rastrick, an English architect recently

Upper left: Sandyford Place ranks as one of the finest stone terraces west of Montreal. It was rescued in 1973 by a citizens' action group.
Top: James Street Terrace consists of ten matching rowhouses built 1854–1860.
Bottom: Commercial Block of 1856 is Hamilton's best stone warehouse.

Top: Custom House
Left: Burlington Canal Lighthouse, built by the the Department of Public Works in 1858, was constructed in limestone by stone mason John Brown on the Beach Strip. The traditional, circular lighthouse operated until 1961 and is in the process of being restored, under the guidance of an active citizen's group.

arrived in Hamilton, this magnificent stone structure projects a grandeur and monumentality not often encountered in warehouse design. The masonry of Whirlpool sandstone displays a masterly synthesis of arches, vermiculated corner quoins, pilasters, and brackets, all in the service of the Classical (Renaissance) Revival style. Equally important to the city's commerce was the Custom House, built in 1858–1860, designed first by Frederick Rastrick then adapted by the federal Public Works architect Frederick Rubidge. Of all of Hamilton's public buildings, the Custom House best captured the British passion for the Renaissance Revival, a style that spoke of authority and prestige, particularly with the British coat-of-arms dominating the roofline. George Worthington, the Scottish stonemason who also worked on St. Paul's Presbyterian Church and the Hamilton Waterworks, demonstrated his full mastery of the stonecarver's art in the arched windows, rusticated stonework, and carved window pediments executed in a fine sandstone that was imported from Ohio. An amazing versatility of masonry techniques, from smooth to rusticated to sculpted surfaces, are displayed in this building, an accomplishment that remains unsurpassed in the stone architecture of southwestern Ontario. The growing port activity was also critical to Hamilton's commercial success. When, in 1856, sparks from a steamship ignited the 1837 wooden lighthouse and keeper's dwelling at the entrance to the harbour, the province immediately rebuilt the keeper's house in brick in 1857 and erected a circular stone Burlington Canal Lighthouse in 1858. Standing seventeen metres high, the lighthouse was constructed of squared, rock-faced Queenston limestone by Scottish stonemason John Brown of Thorold, who had worked on the Welland Canal (1845) and subsequently built six similar lighthouses on Lake Huron and Georgian Bay. Sometimes termed the "Imperial tower," these lighthouses featured the familiar tapering cylindrical shape, slit windows, and a lantern above containing a lamp with a Fresnel lens shipped from Paris, France.

The cholera epidemic of 1854 hit Hamilton with devastating results: many people fled; stores closed; and one in every forty inhabitants died. Following the discovery that cholera was linked to polluted water, the city embarked on a new municipal water system, choosing civil engineer Thomas C. Keefer to devise a system whereby water was pumped in from Lake Ontario instead of the adjacent bay. As a result, the new Hamilton Waterworks (Pumphouse) of 1859 was constructed ten kilometres out of town by master mason George Worthington. With the stone pumphouse and adjacent boiler room, the brick-chimneystack, and woodshed, the Waterworks form a rare architectural complex that is Classical in style, but technologically cutting-edge. To support the 90-ton beam engine, and withstand its movement, Keefer provided a massive stone structure, with walls of brownish limestone, one-metre thick and three-storeys high, with a basement and special features of contrasting grey sandstone. A visit inside this "temple of industry" is awe-inspiring: one enters a hall filled with colossal machinery—a pair of giant flywheels flank the interior with their matching nine-metre-long walking beams above. The polished metalwork and elongated, fluted, cast-iron columns merge into a remarkable, gleaming synthesis of machinery and structure. Under the devoted care of retired engineers and the city, the machinery was kept operable so that today a flywheel and walking beam can still be set in motion.

By the late 1850s, Hamilton was hit hard by a depression and finally went bankrupt in 1862—the gaslights were turned off downtown, and the Sheriff closed City Hall and sold the furnishings off at public auction. While the city recovered in the 1870s, the break had brought the era of stone building to an end (except for public buildings and churches). Masons had left or switched to the more fashionable brick, and quarries ceased supplying building stone. Although the city has since lost far more of its stone heritage than any other stone town in southwestern Ontario, the survivors demonstrate the extraordinary level of craftsmanship, design, and dynamism that characterized pre-Confederation Hamilton.

The Hamilton 1859 Pumphouse houses the only surviving operating beam engine in situ in North America. The complex has been restored and is now the Hamilton Museum of Steam and Technology.

St. Marys

Similar to the Grand River, the north branch of the Thames River originated as a glacial spillway whose swift current gradually cut its way down to bedrock. The earliest travellers to its juncture with Trout Creek observed that its shallow depth revealed flats of flag limestone which are still visible today. The first to seize the opportunity to settle here were the brothers James and Thomas Ingersoll from nearby Oxford County—James to buy 337 acres from the Canada Company in 1841 (fourteen years after the Company's John Galt had founded Guelph), and Thomas to build the first saw and grist mills in the next few years. By 1845, over one hundred settlers had arrived at the settlement, most of them of British or American origin who had resided in neighbouring counties. In 1851, J. B. Brown described the place as "… a most lovely spot. The north branch of the Thames here runs over a limestone bed, through beautifully undulating banks; and the stream is clear as crystal … There is an abundance of limestone suitable for building, upon the site of the village." As in other stone towns, the quarrying of St. Marys' Devonian limestone began on a small scale. First, stone was taken from the river beds and banks; then, from individual quarries often owned by stonemasons; and only eventually, from huge pits the size of the town's swimming quarry, owned by large-scale companies.

Around 1850, pioneer Gilbert McIntosh built one of St. Marys' earliest stone dwellings, the McIntosh Cottage, next door to his woollen mill. Solid, unadorned, and durable, the cottage captures a

Left: The Sanderson House, built in 1849 and 1869, illustrates the contrast between the rustic, random-sized stones of the cottage wing and the sophisticated, squared, and coursed ashlar of the later Italianate house. The house has belonged to the Eady publishing family for over a century.

Above: The Tracy House of 1853–1854 captured the essence of Gothic Revival picturesqueness with its steep gables and wilderness setting. In 1926, the Rotary Club of St. Marys acquired the property and presented it to the town. The St. Marys Museum opened in the stone house in 1959.
Right: Despite drastic changes to its riverfront site—the loss of the mill next door, and the construction and subsequent removal of a downtown rail line along the river bank—the 1850 McIntosh Cottage remains comfortably nestled behind its enclosing stone wall, a work of enduring charm.

sense of those rugged frontier days. The limestone masonry work is typically rustic: relatively small stones, randomly coursed, with large lintels and no corner quoins. When landowner George Tracy came to build his new house a few years later, however, he approached the project in a diametrically opposite way—his vision was for a "Castle in the Bush," as it was known locally. Just as James Ingersoll had done the same year, George Tracy purchased four hundred acres from the Canada Company in 1841 (at $2.00 per acre), and planned to make his money by selling town lots in the south ward. Builder-architect Robert Barbour from Rochester, New York, erected the Tracy House in 1853–1854, one of the first estates in St. Marys. Three stonemasons— Frank Anderson, Andrew Knox, and John Whimster, who all went on to build numerous stone structures in town—erected the handsome residence with superior workmanship. The façade is constructed of squared, fifteen-centimetre coursed, local limestone, while the sides and

The Queen Street Block at Victoria Bridge, built originally in the 1850s, bears witness to William Veal Hutton's creation of a stone business sector, which has been sustained over the years although updated in 1884 and again in 1907.

back are of the customary rubblestone. In terms of fashionable style, stately dimensions, and prestigious setting, Tracy's elegant "castle" marked a new level of sophistication in the village.

Another of the founding families, the Huttons (the parents and four sons), emigrated from Hampshire, England, and in 1851 settled permanently in St. Marys, bringing with them considerable financial resources earned from the linen draper and banking trades. The Huttons built in stone, leaving an amazing legacy of seven handsome structures. Only William Veal Hutton's four-storey stone mill has been lost, destroyed by fire in 1921. His own substantial stone house, built in 1858, still stands across the street on the Queen Street Block at

Top: Water Street South, built in 1863, has survived intact, demonstrating the smooth, closely fitted ashlar masonry that was typical of the 1850s and 1860s, not only in St. Marys but throughout southwestern Ontario.
Bottom: St. Marys Junction Station, built in 1858, is one of the last remaining small stations of the Grand Trunk Railway and is recognized as a National Historic Site. The Sarnia line, closed further west at James Street North in 1989, was opened as the Grand Trunk Trail in 1998.

Victoria Bridge. The house originally faced the river with beautiful landscaped grounds in the foreground, while the back was attached to a two-storey commercial stone row he built in 1855. Changes have occurred to the block over time: Hutton's house is now commercial on the ground floor and the front door on the riverside filled in; a rock-faced façade covered the centre section in 1907 (which became the Royal Edward Hotel for eighty years); and the corner building at Water Street acquired a mansard roof in 1884. Hutton further capitalized on his stone complex by building an even larger row across the corner at 6 Water Street South in 1863. It has survived intact, still displaying the beautiful masonry of closely fitted ashlar blocks and compound lintels; eight gracefully arched store windows animate the street façades. His brother Theodore joined in by erecting another stone block at 14 Water Street in the 1860s (on the south side of the Opera House). Taken together, the Huttons' stone architecture virtually transformed St. Marys' earliest business streets.

St. Marys lost out to Stratford as the County Seat in 1853, but gained official village status in 1855, which further encouraged the community's progression towards a permanent settlement. Perhaps the strongest impetus to growth came from the arrival of two Grand Trunk Railway lines into St. Marys by 1858—one connecting Toronto to Sarnia crossing the Thames River (part of a Maine-to-Sarnia system), and the other connecting St. Marys to London (and the Great Western Railway) crossing Trout Creek. This massive undertaking catapulted the local stone building industry into unprecedented production: stone was needed for the Grand Trunk Junction Station, built in 1858 (eighteen by nine metres); the engine house (eighteen by fifty metres), now demolished; and the giant piers for the two viaducts over the rivers. (Just to build the Thames River viaduct required eleven stone piers twenty-one-metres-high—the newspaper advertised for twenty masons, fifty quarrymen, and one hundred labourers.) The Junction Station, located on the outskirts of town, once functioned as the centre of a small railway settlement, but now stands vacant in the fields, a rare survivor of the mighty Grand Trunk Railway system. It represents the prototype station of well-built masonry walls; wide, overhanging eaves; and arched

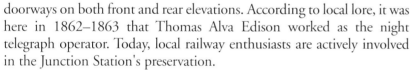

doorways on both front and rear elevations. According to local lore, it was here in 1862–1863 that Thomas Alva Edison worked as the night telegraph operator. Today, local railway enthusiasts are actively involved in the Junction Station's preservation.

Stone, said to be left over from the Sarnia viaduct, went into building the John Sparling House, erected in 1858 at the eastern limits of St. Marys. John Sparling, a local magistrate and the first clerk of the village, is said to have employed the architect W. Graeme Tompkins to design a cottage of great charm. Its label mouldings over the windows, steep roof, and undulating bargeboards distinguish it as a delightful Tudor version of the Gothic Revival style. That the measure of the man proved not as solid as his building came out when he apparently absconded with some Methodist church funds and a parishioner's wife.

The first settlers of St. Marys were mostly a mixture of Scottish, Irish and English stock, who by the 1850s had all built churches for

Upper left: St. James Anglican Church, built originally in 1857–1859 in local limestone, is St. Marys' oldest stone church. The church, with its 1880s belltower, 1907 stone Parish Hall, and spacious grounds form a lovely historic ensemble.

Above and left: The John Sparling House, built of local limestone in 1858, is believed to be the work of architect W. Graeme Tompkins who was associated with the Grand Trunk Railway. Magistrate Sparling was known as "Potato John" for sentencing local miscreants to plant potatoes on the field behind his house.

Above: The MacKay House, dated 1865, with its steep Gothic Revival gable, delicate bargeboard, and amazingly tall finial, imparts a joyous quality to the solid, well-proportioned structure, a combination not uncommon in St. Marys' stone houses.

Right: The Grant House was built by father and son stonemasons in 1863. Hailing from Elgin, Morayshire, Scotland, Alexander and John Grant built a quintessential Ontario Cottage using traditional Scottish masonry.

their own denominations. The only stone church to survive from these early years is St. James Anglican Church built 1857–1859. Originally, the Gothic Revival church was a simple, rectangular building, built mainly by parishioners. However, in the 1880s, when church building was at its height in St. Marys, local architect William Williams provided new plans for St. James to raise the roof, erect a square tower and belfry, and reinforce the walls with buttresses. A parish hall was added in 1907. The spacious site, a gift from James Ingersoll in 1852, has allowed the church to grow and sustain a continuous presence for 150 years.

By 1861, St. Marys boasted a population of 2,728 and 450 dwellings, sixty-seven of which were built of stone. In 1864, it became incorporated as a town. This enabled St. Marys to withdraw from Perth County the following year. Politically independent and now flourishing as a grain-shipping market, the town was in its heyday. In 1865, it built the stone-arched Victoria Bridge over the Thames River (restored and updated in 1984). Residents began building fine houses, many of stone, from small to large.

Left: Sanderson House displays elaborate woodworking in its decorative porches and eaves, not surprising from an owner who was a carpenter by training and then later a lumberyard owner.
Above: Westover Park was built in 1867 for the brothers Joseph and William Veal Hutton. Echoes of the earlier Tracy House are evident in its form and Gothic Revival style. Both were designed by architect Robert Barbour. In 1983, the Hutton estate became the Westover Inn.

Along Thomas Street on the west bank of the Thames, a number of architects, builders, and stonemasons erected their homes. One of the oldest is the Grant House, built in 1863 by Scottish stonemasons Alexander Grant and his son, John. Typically, the limestone was squared and evenly coursed and the structure strengthened by large lintel blocks and corner quoins. The fine proportions and recessed panelled doorway with moulded pilasters show the extra care taken in its construction. Larger houses were built more frequently on higher ground. In the west ward, another early pioneer was James MacKay, whose enterprising spirit ran the gamut of frontier careers, from store owner to a mail and stage coach business. In 1865, the MacKay House arose on the Queen Street West hill, a testimonial in stone to the owner's entrepreneurial success and fashionable good taste. Meanwhile, across the river valley on the Queen Street East hill, another prospering businessman, John Sanderson, was erecting

The Opera House was built in 1880 for the Independent Order of Odd Fellows. The rock-faced stone, attenuated Gothic windows, and Scottish Baronial battlements and turrets form a unique landmark. It is now converted into apartments.

his prestigious home, the Sanderson House, in 1869. But the Irish-born Sanderson kept his first home of 1849, the attached one-storey cottage, as a wing and perhaps also as a graphic reminder of his rise from carpenter to lumberyard owner. The difference in stonework tells the story of how masonry techniques had developed over those twenty years. This later Italianate house is thought to be constructed by James Elliott, stonemason for the Opera House. Ornate verandas and a stone wall set the property off to its best advantage. Meanwhile, on the west side of the river at Westover Park, the Hutton brothers, Joseph and William, were building their retirement estate in 1867 (while still in their forties, for "the quiet afternoon of [their] life"). Westover Park, designed by Robert Barbour, architect of the Tracy House, used a similar double-gabled form with matching bargeboard, yet updated this grander home to the 1860s with a bay window and larger ashlar masonry. The Huttons' lifelong horticultural passion came out in the landscaping of seven acres of gardens and lawn, augmented by a spectacular conservatory, said to be "difficult to equal in Canada." Happily, the "quiet afternoon of [their] life" lasted about forty years until 1910, when the property was bequeathed to their niece Mina. Mina carried on the Hutton legacy of steward and builder until her death in 1938. After a number of interim uses, Westover Park became an inn in 1983.

In the last quarter of the nineteenth century, brick became the dominant building material throughout Ontario. It was not uncommon in St. Marys to find upscale Victorian houses of brick, yet stone still remained deeply rooted in the town's psyche. St. Marys' pride in using its local stone continued longer than in other stone centres. Rock-faced tooling of local limestone became fashionable as a decorative treatment—imported stone was kept to a minimum. Near the end of the century, St. Marys' stone town image became firmly entrenched with the building of a series of high-profile, landmark buildings of local limestone: the Opera House; the Town Hall; and the two glorious churches whose steeples still dominate the North Ward hilltop—the First Presbyterian Church (1881) and Holy Name of

Mary Catholic Church (1892). Even the federal government carried on this local tradition by using St. Marys' stone in its 1907 Post Office and Customs building. Perhaps the most extraordinary of all these monuments is the Opera House, erected in 1880 by stonemason James Elliott in between the Huttons' formal stone rows on Water Street South. It was the novel idea of the St. Marys Independent Order of Odd Fellows to combine three different functions into a wonderfully innovative building: their private lodge premises were on the top floor; an 800-seat theatre on the middle two floors; and stores at ground level. Designed by architect Silas Weekes of London (a lodge member), this dramatic, castellated Victorian Gothic monument was the much-beloved entertainment focus of the town for the next forty years. The St. Marys Lions Club saved the Opera House from demolition in 1986 with help from federal and provincial grants. Could it be that these rock-faced turrets inspired the magnificent new Town Hall of 1891? Architect George W. Gouinlock of Toronto took these picturesque forms to new heights by incorporating them into a lively Romanesque Revival design. Constructed by John Elliott, son of the mason who built the Opera House, the Town Hall features a tall, corner belfry tower, turrets, and sensuously textured stone walls that flow around corners. When completed, an observer stated—and it still holds true—the St. Marys Town Hall is a "credit to any city in the Dominion."

"Born of water and stone," St. Marys has treasured these gifts of nature. The town has always incorporated the rivers into daily life and has spanned them in many different ways over the years. Builders throughout the nineteenth century stayed loyal to their own limestone, not looking to import building stone when it became fashionable elsewhere. Perhaps the town's early political independence (withdrawing from Perth County in 1865) and its role as a major supplier of building stone to western Ontario helped give it individuality and cohesion. With most of its stone heritage still in use, or adapted to new uses when necessary, St. Marys today is justly proud of its "stone town" identity.

The St. Marys Town Hall, designed by architect George W. Gouinlock and built in 1891, still serves the same function today. Its colourful Romanesque Revival features and rock-faced limestone façades with sandstone trim create an unusually engaging civic landmark.

Afterword

The years of the 1850s through the 1870s marked the heyday for building in local stone in southwestern Ontario. The period saw the transformation of pioneer settlements into stable, responsible communities under the leadership of the first- and second-generation settlers. By the 1850s, the founding fathers had accumulated sufficient wealth to create the type of community they had envisioned for posterity. It was a vision that relied heavily on the cultural preferences they had brought with them: for stone and certain architectural fashions. The stonemasons of this founding era similarly had brought with them the high level of the skills and craftsmanship that were the traditions of their homelands.

Beginning in the 1880s, there was a shift in the building industry in southwestern Ontario. Brick had become more fashionable and cheaper; where it wasn't produced locally, it could be easily transported by rail. Stone was typically used for high-profile public structures such as government buildings and churches. In these cases, the use of imported stone—sandstone from the Credit Valley, for example— became a popular trend. As the demand for locally quarried stone dropped off, there wasn't enough business to sustain those quarries specializing in building stone; some had already run out of usable stone. As a result, building in stone became more expensive; younger masons generally turned to brick or moved on. Stylistically, there was a change in favour of the more rustic, rock-faced masonry that did not require the high level of skill of first-generation stonemasons.

Exceptions to these trends seemed to concentrate in those areas where stone construction was the most popular and where stone was still widely available. The stone towns of Fergus, Guelph, Galt, and St. Marys carried on building in local stone throughout the nineteenth century and, in some cases, into the first decade of the twentieth century. Imitation cast stone became competitive after the turn of the century.

By then, the use of reinforced concrete and steel skeletons began to take over, and stone was reduced mainly to a facing material, with Queenston limestone being among the most popular. Modern technology had displaced traditional stone construction; in effect, it was the final step in bringing to a close this chapter in Ontario's architectural history.

Appendix: Heritage Status

Below is a list of the buildings included in this book, by chapter, with information on their heritage status.

Listed means that a building is recognized for its heritage value by being placed on a municipal heritage inventory. Listing a building does not carry with it any obligations or restrictions; it is for information purposes only. Designated buildings are also included in the inventory.

Designated is a formal procedure under the *Ontario Heritage Act* whereby a municipal council passes a bylaw recognizing a property's significance to the community. Designation protects heritage buildings against demolition or inappropriate alterations. The local municipality also has on file the Reasons for Designation, which provides additional information about the building.

Provincial Historical Plaque commemorates a building, person, or event considered to be of provincial significance by the current Ontario Heritage Trust or its preceding government historical agencies. The *Ontario Heritage Act* allows the minister of culture to prohibit demolition of a provincially significant building.

National Historic Site and Plaque indicates that the building, person, or event is considered to be of national significance by the Historic Sites and Monuments Board of Canada.

Chapter One: The Niagara Peninsula

Nelles Manor, 126 Main Street West; Grimsby; Designated; Provincial Historical Plaque for Lieutenant-Colonel Robert Nelles; private home

Brown-Jouppien House, 1317 Pelham Road, St. Catharines; Designated; private home

St. Mark's Anglican Church, 41 Byron Street, Niagara-on-the-Lake; Listed; Provincial Historical Plaque; still in original use

Davis-Prest House, 1755 York Road, Queenston; Designated; private home

Davis-Elder House, 1717 York Road, Queenston; Designated; private home

Mackenzie House, 1 Queenston Street, Queenston; Listed; Provincial Historical Plaque commemorating William Lyon Mackenzie's first publication of the *Colonial Advocate* at this location in 1824; now the Mackenzie Printery and Newspaper Museum, open to the public (contact 905-262-5676), owned by the Niagara Parks Commission

Willowbank, 14487 Niagara Parkway (at the corner of Dee Road), Queenston; Designated; Provincial Historical Plaque; National Historic Site and Plaque; now the School of Restoration Arts at Willowbank, open to the public, provides lectures, tours, and special events (contact 905-262-1239)

Ruthven, 243 Highway 54, Cayuga; Designated; Provincial Historical Plaque, Ruthven Park National Historic Site, open to the public, provides tours, lectures, and special events (contact 905-772-0560)

Chapter Two: Fergus and Elora

Argo Block, 100–124 St. Andrew Street West, southwest corner at St. David Street, Fergus; Listed; in commercial use

Marshall Block, 101 St. Andrew Street West, northwest corner of St. David Street, Fergus; Listed; in commercial use

St. Andrew's Presbyterian Church, 325 St. George Street West at James Square, Fergus; Listed; Provincial Historical Plaque; still in original use

Former manse, St. Andrew's Presbyterian Church, 125 St. George Street East, Fergus; Listed; private home

Rennie Cottage, 396 St. Andrew Street East, Fergus; Designated; private home

Former Beatty Brothers Foundry, 100–105 Queen Street West, Fergus; Listed; open to the public as the Fergus Market (contact 519-843-5221)

Former Wellington County House of Industry and Refuge, 0536 Wellington Road 18, (between Fergus and Elora); Listed; National Historic Site and Plaque; open to the public, Wellington County Museum and Archives, exhibitions and research (contact 519-846-0916, ext. 221)

Elora Mill, 77 Mill Street West, Elora; Designated; open as the Elora Mill Inn (contact 866-713-5672)

Shops, 42–56 Mill Street West, Elora; Listed; in commercial use

Drew House, 120 Mill Street East, Elora; Designated; open as a bed and breakfast, and for special events (contact 519-846-2226)

Inglebrook, 255 Geddes Street, Elora; Designated; private home

Former Drill Shed, 23 High Street, Elora; Designated; National Historic Site and Plaque; now an LCBO store

Knox Presbyterian Church, 55 Church Street; Listed; continues in original use

CHAPTER THREE: GUELPH

Wellington County Courthouse, 74 Woolwich Street, Guelph; Designated; continues in original use

Guelph Town Hall and Market House, 59 Carden Street, Guelph; Designated; Provincial Historical Plaque; currently functions as the Guelph City Hall

Medical Hall, 12 Wyndham Street North, Guelph; Designated; continues in commercial use

Alma Building, 127–135 Wyndham Street, Guelph; Listed; continues in commercial use

Wellington Building, 147–159 Wyndham Street North, Guelph; Designated; continues in commercial use

St. Andrew's Presbyterian Church, 161 Norfolk Street, Guelph; Listed; continues in original use

St. George's Anglican Church, 99 Woolwich Street, Guelph; Listed; continues in original use

Church of Our Lady of Immaculate Conception, 28 Norfolk Street, Guelph; Listed; National Historic Site; continues in original use

Perry-Scroggie House, 15 Oxford Street, Guelph; Designated; private home

McCrae Birthplace Museum, 108 Water Street, Guelph; Designated; National Historic Site commemorating the birthplace of doctor-soldier-poet Lieutenant-Colonel John McCrae; city museum, open to the public (contact 519-836-1482)

McTague Cottages, 346 and 348 Woolwich Street, Guelph; Listed; private homes

House-of-Heads, 96–98 Water Street, Guelph; Designated; now a two-family private home

Matthew Bell House, 40 Albert Street, Guelph; Designated; private home

264 Woolwich Street, Guelph; Designated; currently under renovation

Ker Cavan, 20 Stuart Street, Guelph; Designated; now a two-family private home

Wyoming, 67 Queen Street, Guelph; Listed; private home; central tower recently restored

CHAPTER FOUR: WATERLOO REGION

David Weber House, 69 Biehn Drive, Kitchener; Designated; private home

Adam Ferrie Jr. House, 39 Doon Valley Drive, Kitchener; Listed; Kitchener Historical plaque; private home

Woolner House, 748 Zeller Drive, Kitchener; Designated; private home

Brubacher House, Columbia Street West, University of Waterloo, North Campus, Waterloo; Designated; open to the public as a Mennonite house museum, operated by Conrad Grebel University College and the Mennonite Historical Society of Ontario (contact 519-886-3855)

Swope House, 52 Hill Street, West Montrose, Woolwich Township; Designated; private home

West Montrose Schoolhouse, 1060 Rivers Edge Drive, West Montrose, Woolwich Township; Listed; now converted to a private home

Joseph Zehr House, 1138 Snyders Road, Baden, Wilmot Township; Designated; descendants of the original owner still occupy the home

Moses Hostetler House, 1145 Christner Road, New Hamburg, Wilmot Township; Designated; private home

CHAPTER FIVE: CAMBRIDGE

Kirkmichael, 16 Byng Avenue, Cambridge (Galt); Listed; private home

Dickson Mill, 4 Park Hill Road West, Cambridge (Galt); Listed; mill now converted into a restaurant

Trinity Anglican Church, 12 Blair Road., Cambridge (Galt); Listed; in original use

Galt Town Hall, 46 Dickson Street, Cambridge (Galt); Designated; now Cambridge Historic City Hall

Main Street, north side (nos. 18, 20–22, 26–28, 30–38, 40), Cambridge (Galt); Designated (nos. 18, 20–22) and Listed; still in commercial use

Main Street, south side (nos. 11, 13–39, 51–53, 55–61), Cambridge (Galt); Designated as a Heritage Conservation District; still in commercial use

McDougall Cottage, 69 Grand Avenue South, Cambridge (Galt); Designated; interior known for its hand-painted friezes and *trompe l'oeil* ceilings, now open to the public as a museum, offers mini-exhibits and special events (contact 519-624-8250)

Thornhill, 32 McKenzie Street, Cambridge (Galt); Listed; private home

The Cedars, 45 Blair Road, Cambridge (Galt); Listed; private home, now in the process of being restored

Glen Echo, 27 Carolinian Lane, Cambridge; Designated; private home

Goldie and McCulloch, 64 Grand Avenue South, Cambrige (Galt); Listed; subsequently Babcock and Wilcox; now Southworks Outlet Mall

Galt Foundry and Machine Works, 19–25 Concession Street, Cambridge (Galt); Listed; designation pending; later the Canada Machinery Corporation; now in the process of rehabilitation

Knox Presbyterian Church, 2–6 Grand Avenue. South, adjacent to Queen's Square, Cambridge (Galt); Listed; still in original use

Central Presbyterian Church, 3 Queen's Square, Cambridge (Galt); Designated; still in original use

Dickson Public School, 65 St. Andrews Street, Cambridge (Galt); Designated; still in original use

Former Galt Post Office, 12 Water Street South, Cambridge (Galt); Designated; now converted to commercial use

CHAPTER SIX: PARIS

St. James Anglican Church, 8 Burwell Street at Grand River Street South, Paris; Listed; still in original use

Sowden Home and Dispensary, 7 Burwell Street, Paris; Listed; private residential

Hamilton Place, 165 Grand River Street North, Paris; Designated; private home

Mitchell House, 16 Broadway Street West, Paris; Designated; private home

Bosworth House, 22 Church Street, Paris; Designated; private home

Levi Boughton House, 19 Queen Street, Paris; Listed; private home

22-24 Dumfries Street, Paris; Listed; private residential

Gouinlock House, 42 Broadway Street East, Paris; Designated; private home

Sacred Heart Roman Catholic Church, 17 Washington Street, Paris; Listed; still in original use

Paris Plains Church, 709 Paris Plains Road, Paris; Designated; Provincial Historical Plaque; National Historic Site; open on special occasions

George Brown Farmhouse, 207 West River Road, Paris; Designated; private home

Kilton Cottage, 33 Oak Avenue, Paris; Designated; private home

Deans Farmhouse, 963 Keg Lane Road, Paris; Listed; private home

John Maus House, 289 Pinehurst Road, Paris; Designated; private home

CHAPTER SEVEN: ANCASTER-DUNDAS-FLAMBOROUGH

Union Hotel, 380–386 Wilson Street East, Ancaster; Listed; in commercial use

Fairview, 267 Sulphur Springs Road, Ancaster; Listed; private home

Old Ancaster Mill, 548 Old Dundas Road, Ancaster; Designated; now the Old Ancaster Mill restaurant

St. John's Anglican Church, 272 Wilson Street East, Ancaster; Designated; still in original use

Former Ancaster Township Hall, 310 Wilson Street East, Ancaster; Designated; open for special events

Former Dundas Town Hall, 60 Main Street, Dundas; Designated; accommodates some local services for Dundas for the amalgamated City of Hamilton, and special events

Wood-Dale, 35 Cross Street, Dundas; Designated, in the Cross-Melville Heritage Conservation District; private home

Foxbar, 7 Overfield Street, Dundas; Designated; private home

James Scott House, 146 Park Street West, Dundas; Listed; private home

250–252 King Street West, Dundas; Listed, private home

Griffin House, 201 Main Street South, Waterdown; Listed; private home

Former East Flamborough Township Hall, 25 Mill Street North, Waterdown; Designated; now a public library

Former Weslyan Methodist Church, 21 Mill Street North, Waterdown; Listed; now Church of the Alliance

Stonegates, 193 Highway 8, West Flamborough Village, Flamborough; Listed; private home

Stormont, 218 Highway 8, West Flamborough Village, Flamborough; Listed; private home

Blagdon Farmhouse, 429 7th Concession, Flamborough; Listed; private home

Chapter Eight: Hamilton

Whitehern, 41 Jackson Street West, Hamilton; Designated; Provincial Historical Plaque; National Historic Site and Plaque; now open as a city museum, house museum of the McQuesten family, offers tours, special events (contact 905-546-2018)

Inglewood, 13–15 Inglewood Drive, Hamilton; Listed; private home; now converted into condominiums

Central Public School, 75 Hunter Street West; Designated; Provincial Historical Plaque; still in original use

St. Paul's Presbyterian Church, 64 James Street South, Hamilton; Designated; Provincial Historical Plaque; National Historic Site and Plaque; still in original use

James Street Stone Terrace, 142–160 James Street South, Hamilton; Designated; originally private homes; currently in commercial use

Sandyford Place, 35–43 Duke Street, Hamilton; Designated; National Historic Site and Plaque; private homes; now converted into condominiums

Commercial Block, 63–73 MacNab Street North, Hamilton; Designated; still in commercial use

Hamilton Custom House, 51 Stuart Street, Hamilton; Designated; National Historic Site and Plaque; now open to the public as the Ontario Workers, Arts and Heritage Centre, offers tours, programs, and exhibitions (contact 905-522-3003)

Burlington Canal Lighthouse, 1159 Beach Boulevard, Hamilton; Designated; now in process of restoration

Hamilton Waterworks (1859), 900 Woodward Avenue, Hamilton; Designated; National Historic Site and Plaque; now open to the public as a city museum, the Museum of Steam and Technology, offers tours with an operating pump and flywheel, exhibitions (contact 905-546-4797)

Chapter Nine: St. Marys

McIntosh Cottage, 226 Thames Street (at the St. Maria Street extension), St. Marys; Listed; private home

Tracy House, 177 Church Street South, St. Marys; Designated; now open to the public as the St. Marys Museum, offers tours, special events, research material (contact 519-284-3556)

83–91 Queen Street East at Victoria Bridge, St. Marys; Listed; still in commercial use

M&M Building, 6 Water Street, St. Marys; Designated; still in commercial use

St. Marys Junction Station, 480 Glass Street, St. Marys; Designated; National Historic Site and Plaque; currently vacant

John Sparling House, 615 Queen Street East, St. Marys; Listed; private home with antique store

St. James Anglican Church, 65 Church Street South, St. Marys; Listed; still serves original use

Grant House, 181 Thomas Street South, St. Marys; Designated; private home

MacKay House, 144 Queen Street West, St. Marys; Designated; private home

Sanderson House, 252 Queen Street East, St. Marys; Designated; private home

Westover Park, 300 Thomas Street South, St. Marys; Listed; originally private home; now open to the public as the Westover Inn, (contact 519-284-2977)

Opera House, 12 Water Street South, St. Marys; Designated; originally housed the opera house, IOOF headquarters, and stores; now converted to condominiums

St. Marys Town Hall, 175 Queen Street East, St. Marys; Designated; still in original use

BIBLIOGRAPHY

GENERAL

Andreae, Christopher. *Lines of the Country: An Atlas of Railway and Waterway History in Canada.* Erin, ON: Boston Mills Press, 1997.

Angus, Margaret. *The Old Stones of Kingston: Its Buildings Before 1867.* Toronto: University of Toronto Press, 1966.

Ashenburg, Katherine. *Going to Town: Architectural Walking Tours in Southern Ontario.* Toronto: Macfarlane Walter & Ross, 1996.

Blake, Verschoyle Benson, and Ralph Greenhill. *Rural Ontario.* Toronto: University of Toronto Press, 1969.

Blumenson, John. *Ontario Architecture: A Guide to Styles and Building Terms, 1784 to the Present.* Markham, ON: Fitzhenry & Whiteside, 1990.

Brunskill, R. W. *Illustrated Handbook of Vernacular Architecture.* Third edition, London: faber & faber, 1987.

Byers, Mary, and Margaret McBurney. *The Governor's Road: Early Buildings and Families from Mississauga to London.* Toronto: University of Toronto Press, 1982.

Clifton-Taylor, Alec, and A. S. Ireson. *English Stone Building.* Revised edition, London: Victor Gollancz, 1994.

Couling, Gordon. "Ontario Stone." Unpublished manuscript. Gordon Couling Collection. University of Guelph Library, Archives and Special Collections, Guelph, ON.

Cruickshank, Tom. *Old Ontario Houses: Traditions in Local Architecture.* Willowdale, ON: Firefly Books, 2000.

Dahms, Fred. *Beautiful Ontario Towns.* Toronto: James Lorimer, 2001.

Gentilcore, R. Louis, and C. Grant Head. *Ontario History in Maps.* Toronto: University of Toronto Press, 1984.

Greenhill, Ralph, Ken MacPherson, and Douglas Richardson. *Ontario Towns.* Ottawa: Oberon, 1972.

Kalman, Harold. *A History of Canadian Architecture.* 2 vols. Toronto: Oxford University Press, 1994.

MacRae, Marion, and Anthony Adamson. *Cornerstones of Order: Courthouses and Town Halls of Ontario, 1784–1914.* Toronto: Clarke Irwin, 1983.

———. *Hallowed Walls: Church Architecture of Upper Canada.* Toronto, Vancouver: Clarke, Irwin, 1975.

———. *The Ancestral Roof: Domestic Architecture of Upper Canada.* Toronto and Vancouver: Clarke, Irwin, 1963.

McArthur, Glenn, and Annie Szamosi. *William Thomas Architect, 1799–1860.* N.p.: Archives of Canadian Art, 1996.

McIlwraith, Thomas F. *Looking for Old Ontario: Two Centuries of Landscape Change.* Toronto: University of Toronto Press, 1997.

McKee, Harley J. *Introduction to Early American Masonry: Stone, Brick, Mortar and Plaster.* Washington, DC: Preservation Press, 1973.

Mikel, Robert. *Ontario House Styles: The Distinctive Architecture of the Province's 18th and 19th Century Homes.* Toronto: James Lorimer, 2004.

Miller, Willet G. *The Limestones of Ontario.* Bureau of Mines, 1904. Part II. Toronto: L. K. Cameron, 1904.

Moffat, Ruth. *Stone Houses: Stepping Stones from the Past.* Erin, ON: Boston Mills Press, 1984.

Smith, W. H. *Canada: Past, Present and Future.* 2 vols. Toronto: Thomas Maclear, 1852.

Spalding-Smith, Fiona, and Barbara A. Humphreys. *Legacy in Stone: The Rideau Corridor.* Erin, ON: Boston Mills Press, 1999.

INDIVIDUAL TOWNS OR AREAS

Ancaster, Dundas, and Flamborough

Green, Patricia, Maurice H. Green, Sylvia Wray, and Robert Wray. . . . *And They Came to East Flamborough: A Celebration of East Flamborough Township's Pre-Confederation Heritage.* Waterdown–East Flamborough Heritage Society, 1997.

———. *From West Flamborough's Storied Past: A Celebration of West Flamborough Township's Heritage.* Waterdown–East Flamborough Heritage Society, 2003.

Grimwood, Paul, ed. *Ancaster's Heritage: A History of Ancaster Township.* Vol. II. Ancaster, ON: Ancaster Township Historical Society, 1998.

Norris, Darrell A. *Beyond Paradise: Building Dundas, 1793–1950.* Ed. Linda Helson. Local Architectural Conservation Advisory Committee of the Town of Dundas, 1996.

Woodhouse, Roy T., and Thomas W. D. Farmer, ed. *Ancaster's Heritage.* Vol. I. Ancaster Township Historical Society, 1970.

Cambridge

Bloomfield, G. T. *Industrial Buildings and Vernacular Housing.* N.p.: SSAC Field Guide, 1984.

City of Cambridge. *Heritage Properties Inventory.* Cambridge, ON: 2002.

Couling, Gordon. *Our Heritage in Stone.* Cambridge, ON: Heritage Cambridge, 1978.

———. "Stone Masonry in Waterloo County." *Waterloo Historical Society Journal*, 63 (1975), 32–43.

Dilse, Paul. *A Remarkable Heritage: Programmes and Policies for Heritage Conservation in Cambridge, Ontario.* Cambridge, ON: Heritage Cambridge and the City of Cambridge, 1981.

McLaughlin, Kenneth. *Cambridge: The Making of a Canadian City.* N.p.: Windsor Publications, 1987.

Young, James. *Reminiscences of the Early History of Galt and the Settlement of Dumfries in the Province of Ontario.* Toronto: Hunter, Rose, 1880.

Elora and Fergus

Byerly, A. E. *Fergus or the Fergusson-Webster Settlement with an Extensive History of North-East Nichol.* Elora, ON: Elora Express, 1932–1934.

Connon, John. *Elora: The Early History of Elora and Vicinity.* Waterloo, ON: Wilfred Laurier University Press, 1974.

Hounsell, Sarah, ed. *Inventory of Urban Heritage Buildings: Township of Centre Wellington.* Heritage Centre Wellington, 2004.

Koop, Al. *A Walking Tour Guide of Historic Elora.* Elora Centre for the Arts, n.d.

Mestern, Pat Mattaini. *Fergus: A Scottish Town by Birthright.* Toronto: Natural Heritage/Natural History, 1995.

———. *Looking Back: The Story of Fergus Through the Years.* 2 vols. Fergus, ON: Fergus-Elora News Express, 1983.

Templin, Hugh. *Fergus: The Story of a Little Town.* Fergus, ON: The Fergus News-Record, 1933.

Guelph

City of Guelph LACAC. *Designated Buildings and Structures of Architectural and Historic Interest in the City of Guelph.* 1977–1994.

Johnson, Leo A. *History of Guelph, 1827–1927.* Guelph, ON: Guelph Historical Society, 1977.

Miller, Robert J. "Stone Buildings of Guelph." Master's thesis. Guelph, ON: University of Guelph, 1970.

Stelter, Gilbert A. *49-46 Reading a Community.* http://www.uoguelph.ca/history/urban.html. 1995.

Walking Tours:

Couling, Gordon. *Downtown Walkabout: A Walking Tour of the Central Business District of Guelph.* Guelph, ON: Guelph Arts Council, 1996.

———. *Where Guelph Began: A Walking Tour of the Original Market Square Area.* Guelph, ON: Guelph Arts Council, 1996.

Partridge, Florence. *Altar and Hearth in Victorian Guelph: A Walking Tour of the Area Extending from Essex Street to London Road and Glasgow to Norfolk Street.* Guelph, ON: Guelph Arts Council, 1994.

———. *Brooklyn and the College Hill: A Walking Tour of the Area Extending South from Water Street to the University of Guelph Campus, and West from Mary to Gordon Street.* Guelph, ON: Guelph Arts Council, 1998.

———. *The Slopes of the Speed: A Walking Tour of the Slopes of the Speed River Between Norwich and Macdonell Streets in Guelph.* Guelph, ON: Guelph Arts Council, 1990.

Hamilton

Bailey, T. Melville, ed. *Dictionary of Hamilton Biography.* Vols. I and II. Hamilton, ON: W. L. Griffin, 1981, 1991.

Gardiner, Herbert. "Hamilton's Stone Age." *Papers and Records of the Wentworth Historical Society,* 11 (1924), 15-36.

Johnston, C. M. *The Head of the Lake: A History of Wentworth County.* Second edition, Hamilton, ON: Wentworth County Council, 1967.

McKay, A.G. *Victorian Architecture in Hamilton.* Architectural Conservancy of Ontario (Hamilton-Niagara Branch), 1967.

Shaw, Susan Evans. *Heritage Treasures: The Historic Homes of Ancaster, Burlington, Dundas, East Flamborough, Hamilton, Stoney Creek, and Waterdown.* Toronto: James Lorimer, 2004.

Weaver, John C. *Hamilton: An Illustrated History.* Toronto: James Lorimer, 1982.

Niagara Peninsula

Grimsby Heritage Advisory Committee (GHAC). *The Nelles Heritage Driving Tour.* N.p.: n.d.

St. Catharines Heritage Committee. *City of St. Catharines Heritage Resource Inventory.* City of St. Catharines, 1996.

Stokes, Peter John. *Early Architecture of the Town and Township of Niagara.* Niagara-on-the-Lake: Niagara Foundation, 1967.

———. *Old Niagara on the Lake.* Toronto: University of Toronto Press, 1971.

Paris

Architectural Conservancy of Ontario, Hamilton Branch. "Cobblestone Buildings of Paris, Ontario." 1966.

County of Brant Heritage Committee. *County of Brant Heritage Driving Tour.* Paris, ON: County of Brant, 2006.

History of Brant County. Toronto: Warner Beers, 1883.

Paris Heritage LACAC. *Paris: An Architectural Walking Tour.* Paris, ON: County of Brant, 1999.

Smith, Donald A. *At the Forks of the Grand: Twenty Historical Essays on Paris, Ontario.* Vol. 1. Paris, ON: Paris Centennial Committee, 1956.

Snelgren Jr., Olaf William, Cary Lattin, and Robert W. Frasch. *Cobblestone Landmarks of New York State.* Syracuse, NY: Syracuse University Press, 1978.

St. Marys

Johnston, W. Stafford, and Hugh J. M. Johnston. *History of Perth County to 1967.* Stratford: County of Perth, 1967.

Pfaff, Larry. *Historic St. Marys.* St. Marys: J. W. Eedy, n.d.

Pfaff, L. R., and C. M. Pfaff. *Limestone Legacy in St. Marys: The Story of the Huttons, Millers, and Gentlemen.* Thames Label & Litho, 1998.

Wilson, L. W., and L. R. Pfaff. *Early St. Marys: A History in Old Photographs from Its Founding to 1914.* Erin, ON: Boston Mills Press, 1981.

Waterloo Area

Beasley, David. *Richard Beasley and the German Companies.* Simcoe, ON: Davus, 2005.

Bloomfield, Elizabeth. *Waterloo Township Through Two Centuries.* Waterloo, ON: Waterloo Historical Society, 1995.

Frets, J. Winfield. *The Waterloo Mennonites: A Community in Paradox.* Waterloo, ON: Wilfrid Laurier University Press, 1989.

Region of Waterloo Heritage Planning Advisory Committee. *Historical Driving Tours in Waterloo Region.* Region of Waterloo, n.d.

GLOSSARY

ARCHES

arch: a curved construction that spans an opening.

Arch shapes:
round: a semi-circle.
semi-elliptical: a three-to-five centred arch.
segmental: less than a semi-circle.
ogee: a double (reverse) curve.
pointed: having a point at its apex.
flat: horizontal.
voussoirs: wedge-shaped masonry units whose central voussoir is the keystone. In peacock-fan voussoirs, the individual stones become progressively attenuated, such as in Glen Echo, Cambridge.

ARCHITECTURAL STYLES

The Oxford Dictionary describes architectural style as a definite type of architecture distinguished by special characteristics of structure and ornament. The nineteenth century saw a progression of styles that are characterized by the following features (dates are approximate).
Georgian (1784–1860): symmetry, centre-hall, often two-storey (for example, Nelles Manor, Grimsby).
Regency (1830–1860*)*: houses—often with hip roofs, large French windows, verandas (for example, Wood-Dale, Dundas).
Greek Revival (1830–1860): inspired by the Greek temple, classical columns, pediments (for example, Ruthven, Cayuga).
Gothic Revival (1830–1900): pointed arch, curvilinear bargeboard in gables, finials, elaborate chimneys, battlements, label mouldings (for example, Inglewood, Hamilton).
Classical Revival, including *Renaissance Revival* (1840–1865): symmetrical form with corner quoins, pilasters, and carved pedimental window heads (for example, Sandyford Place, Hamilton).
Italianate Revival (1860–1890): large brackets—sometimes paired; wide overhanging eaves, tall proportions, round and segmental arched windows, decorative window heads (for example, Inglebrook, Elora).
Second Empire (1860–1900): mansard roof (double-pitched with a steep lower slope), dormers, slate roof, iron cresting (for example, Wyoming in Guelph and the Marshall Block in Fergus).

Romanesque Revival (1880–1900): round, often-oversized arches; turrets; rounded corners; buttresses; and rock-faced stone (for example, Town Hall, St. Marys).

BUILDING STONE

Building stone in southwestern Ontario consists mainly of the following:
cobbles: glacial- or water-rounded stones (1/2" to 10" in size, according to geologists), that are laid in mortar at right angles to the wall, forming a cobblestone veneer
fieldstone: loose, unfinished stone found on the surface or in the soil.
freestone: any fine-grained stone, such as limestone or sandstone, that can be quarried or worked easily, especially one that cuts well in all directions.
granite: an igneous rock that is very hard and coarse grained, composed mainly of quartz, feldspar, and mica or other coloured minerals (granite is found as fieldstone in southwestern Ontario).
limestone: a sedimentary rock formed chiefly by the accumulation of organic remains, such as shells and coral, and consisting mainly of calcium carbonate.
sandstone: a sedimentary rock consisting of sand, usually quartz, cemented together by various substances such as silica, clay, or calcium carbonate.

CHURCH FEATURES

ambulatory: corridor around the apse; or covered walk of a cloister.
apse: semi-circular or semi-polygonal structure that contains the altar.
buttress: an exterior mass of masonry set at an angle to or bonded into a wall for support.
clerestory: upper storey of nave with windows.
nave: principal space or middle aisle of a church.
radiating chapels: chapels projecting off from the ambulatory.
spire: slender, pointed construction surmounting a building.
spire, broached: polygonal spire surmounting a square tower.
steeple: a tall, ornamental tower of a series of diminishing storeys.
transept: transverse portion of the nave.

triforium: storey above the nave, usually without windows.

CLASSICAL ORDERS

colonette: small column.
column: composed of a base, shaft, capital, and entablature.
Corinthian: fluted column with acanthus leaves on capital.
Doric: fluted column with plain "cushion" capital.
entablature: in classical architecture, the upper part above the capital comprising the architrave (the beam that spans from column to column—the lowermost section; *see also* Window and doorway features); the frieze (a decorative band—the middle section); and the cornice (a moulded projection—the uppermost section).
Ionic: fluted column with volutes (spiral, scroll-like ornaments) on capital.
pilaster: shallow, flattened "column," part of wall.
Tuscan: of Roman origin, not fluted, with plain capital similar to Doric.

FACADE FEATURES

bargeboard or vergeboard: ornamental board or decorative woodwork fixed to the edges of a gable roof; also called gingerbread.
bay: opening in the facade (window or door) that is used to calculate the width of the building, as in three-bays wide.
bracket: curved support that projects from the wall and is attached under the eaves, as in bracketed eaves.
corbel: stone projecting from wall to support a weight.
dentil: square block set in frieze below cornice.
quoin: larger masonry block used at corners or edges of wall for strengthening.
veranda: covered porch or balcony on exterior of building.

MASONRY

ashlar: building stone that has been squared and dressed and laid with close joints.
dressed: squared on all four sides and smoothed on the face.
mortar: historically, a mixture of sand, slaked lime (hydraulic lime), and water used for bonding a masonry wall.
pointing: the filling of the mortar joints in masonry.

Tooled finishes include:
hammer-dressed: lightly textured surface.
rock-faced or *quarry-faced:* natural face of the stone.
rusticated: heavily textured surface; also cut stone with strongly emphasized recessed joints.

vermiculated: wandering, wavy lines as if caused by the movement of worms.
Types of construction:
irregular coursed: continuous levels but different-sized stones.
random coursed: discontinuous horizontal pattern.
regular coursed: continuous levels of same-sized stones.
rhythmic broken coursed: continuous horizontal course with two or three small blocks inserted into vertical space between blocks.
rubblestone: rough, random coursed stonework.

ROOF FEATURES

belfry: bell tower.
bell-cote: small belfry on the ridge of a church roof.
belvedere: rooftop pavilion from which a view can be enjoyed.
cupola: dome-shaped structure set on a circular base on the ridge of a roof and opened up by windows.
finial: ornamental, vertical projection, often at the peak of a gable roof.
lantern: windowed superstructure crowning a roof or a dome.
turret: small tower, characteristically corbelled at the corner.

ROOF TYPES

gable: slopes on two sides.
hipped: slopes on all four sides.
mansard: double-pitched with a steep lower roof.

WINDOW AND DOORWAY FEATURES

architrave: ornamental mouldings around the faces of the jambs (vertical sides) and lintel of a doorway or window (also, a beam in the classical order, *see* entablature).
fanlight: semi-circular, segmental, or semi-elliptical glazed arch above the door.
lintel: horizontal structural member, such as a beam, set over an opening.
moulding: a shaped decorative element that projects slightly from the wall.
pediment: triangular gable end of the roof; also, decorative feature over windows or doors that can be either triangular or curved.
sash: frame for window, double-hung (slides vertically) or casement (pivots).
sidelight: framed area of fixed glass flanking a door or window.
sill: horizontal bottom member of a window.
transom: rectangular glazing above the door.
window head: upper decorative element over a window, such as carved pediments.
window surround: an encircling border or decorative frame.

INDEX

Index